OLDHAM COUNTY

COUNTY

Life

AT THE RIVER'S EDGE

NANCY STEARNS THEISS

Dear Anne —
Thank you for
sharing your story
for our books!
Nancy

Charleston H London

THE
History
PRESS

Published by The History Press
Charleston, SC 29403
www.historypress.net

Cover: *Westport, Ky*, by Oldham County native
and primitive artist Breck Morgan.

All photos are courtesy of the Oldham County Historical Society archives unless
otherwise stated.

First published 2010

Manufactured in the United States

ISBN 978.1.59629.862.0

Library of Congress CIP data applied for.

Contents

CONTENTS

Acknowledgements

I have enjoyed the opportunity to put together these stories for the *Louisville Courier-Journal* and would like to thank editors Veda Morgan and Carolyn Yetter for their help. Thanks to Ryan Finn at The History Press for quick responses to my questions. Special thanks to the Oldham County Historical Society genealogist, Dot Carraco, for proofing the manuscript. The archives and history of these stories would not be possible without the following: the Oldham County Board of Directors—Bob Martin, Kevin Eldridge, Sally Landes, Raymond Simpson, Lee Clore, Oren Clore, Shirley Orr, Traci Leet, Tracy Johnson, Marian Klein-Koehler, Alex Babey, Duane Murner, Harry Bell and Denia Crosby. Also, there have been numerous individuals who have given exceptional volunteer time to the history center, in particular Dottie and Bill Lammlein, June Taylor, Genie and Bob Fortunato, Faye Owen and Peggy Burge. A special thanks to the Peyton Samuel Head Trust, Virginia and Howard Mahan Trust, the Oldham County Fiscal Court and the Oldham County History Center Gala Committee, under the direction of Karen Eldridge, for providing funds that help to manage the archives and programs at the Oldham County History Center. In addition, history center staff members Pam Fields, Jan Jasper, Dot Carraco and Martina Gonzalez provide friendly service to the folks who are in search of their history. Last but not least, a very special thanks to my very special family, Jim, Jessie and Denny Gray and Jimmy Dan, and to my mentors, Dr. John Keedy, Dr. Dave Maurer, Dr. Louis Krumholz and Aldo Leopold.

Part of the proceeds from this book benefit the Oldham County Historical Society.

Introduction

The Mason-Dixon line was originally forged when two surveyors, Charles Mason and Jeremiah Dixon, were hired to settle a boundary dispute between the Calvert and Penn families to distinguish Maryland and Pennsylvania lands. Fifty years later, it was used in the Missouri Compromise of 1820 to distinguish slave states from free states. Basically, the Mason-Dixon line referred to the states that were located from south of the Ohio River to its mouth at the Mississippi and then west thirty-six degrees and thirty minutes north, according to an online geographical definition provided by Matt Rosenburg.

The Ohio River was a corridor for the new frontier, and Oldham County was certainly an attraction for new families. After the Revolutionary War, English families brought with them their slaves and settled in the fertile river bottom areas and bluegrass ridgelines. Germans started vineyards and vegetable farms, and in 1854, with the advent of the railroad, Oldham County prospered by shipping produce and livestock via the rails.

Although declaring late for the Union during the Civil War, Kentucky was a slave state that participated heavily in slave trade and replenished the slave markets of the Deep South. Counties along the river, like Oldham, had easy access for trading, selling and shipping slaves. The Ohio River became a link in the Underground Railroad path for slaves escaping to the North, and it became a link in the bonds of slavery for others, as people were sent downriver to replenish the slave markets in the Natchez Trace.

As the Civil War passed, local African Americans families struggled for their civil rights. Other Oldham County residents, such as pioneer filmmaker D.W. Griffith and children's author Annie Fellows Johnston, depicted Oldham County as a genteel southern landscape of comfort and tradition. Local natives became storybook figures in the "Little Colonel" series of children's books by Johnston, and the pastoral scenes that are depicted in Griffith's silent films are often linked to his native home of Oldham County.

The stories and tales of this rich history are recorded through court documents, old newspapers and other artifacts that have been preserved through the efforts of the Oldham County Historical Society.

Many of the stories from this book appeared in a weekly column, "The World Beneath Your Feet," written by the author for the *Louisville Courier-Journal* newspaper. The columns began in June 2007 and explore the history of places, people and events in the area. Some of the oral histories that appear in the stories are taken from interviews that were conducted by the author for the Living Treasures Program at the Oldham County History Center. This program, modeled after one in Santa Fe, New Mexico, explores the lives of mentors ages seventy years and older who have lived in and contributed in various ways to the community.

As the twentieth century progressed, Oldham County remained a rural, agricultural area until the construction of Interstate 71 in 1969. Population shifts changed the structure of the county by the mid-1970s, and by the end of the twentieth century, Oldham County had changed from a farm to a bedroom community, as in nearby Louisville. Today there is a movement to recapture the pastoral landscape with the onset of green space planning and more farmers' markets that would encourage homegrown products. As the world changes, it becomes even more important to preserve the cultural and natural histories that give the distinct flavor and sense of place that ground the well-being and sense of discovery that provide us purpose for day-to-day living.

Part I

MUDDY WATERS

After the Revolutionary War, pioneers begin their westward journeys down the Ohio River, as well as through the Cumberland Gap. Carved out of Virginia, Kentucky was admitted to statehood on June 1, 1792, and it was the first state created west of the Appalachian Mountains. The Ohio River Valley was rich in evidence of artifacts from the many millions of Native Americans who had prospered from the abundant resources. As settlers claimed the fertile farmlands, they found the riverbanks full of mussel shell mounds, flint, pottery shards and arrowheads.

One of the largest Native American settlements, Cahokia, was located just four hours downriver from the area that is today Oldham County. During the 1300s, Cahokia was an important trade center and supported a population of some thirty-two thousand residents. The Shawnee, led by Tecumseh, were the most prevalent tribe during Oldham County's early settlement by Europeans and African Americans. The last Indian attacks occurred in the late 1700s as large portions of land in Oldham County were deeded to surveyors and soldiers who had served in the Revolutionary War. Many of the new settlers were of English descent and were slaveholders. These settlers included the Taylor and Barbour families, Henshaws, Buttons, Speers, Forees, Hitts, Oglesbys, Belknaps, Overstreets and Bennetts, just to mention a few. Small communities, like Westport, sprung up along the banks of the Ohio River and tested the liberties of citizenship that were forged from the new constitution of the United States.

COMMODORE RICHARD TAYLOR

Commodore Richard Taylor was certainly one of the most distinguished pioneers and early citizens of Oldham County. Born in Orange County, Virginia, the commodore married twice and had six sons and five daughters. Taylor was commissioned as a captain in the navy during the Revolutionary War in 1776. He was wounded twice, in the knee and thigh, and retired from active duty in 1781. His vessel, the *Tartar*, was engaged in battle with an English schooner when he received his first wound (the thigh). In November 1781, he was commodore of the *Patriot* in another battle with an English cruiser just outside Chesapeake Bay. The following description of the battle scene was written by Mr. Anderson, who worked with Commodore Taylor and collected historical records, according to Lucien Rule's *Pioneering in Masonry*:

> *The sea was calm and the breeze insufficient to manipulate his vessel. Captain Taylor, therefore, determined to attack the Englishmen in open boats and board and capture her by a hand to hand fight. As his boats approached the enemy, they were the target for volley after volley from the guns of the British, but without damage to any of them. The American seamen were enthusiastic and felt that victory was within their grasp, when one of Captain Taylor's sailors, making mock of the British fire, exclaimed, "Why don't you elevate your mettle?" This hint to elevate the breeches of their guns was acted on and a volley of grape shot fired into Captain Taylor's boat, defeated his bold plan of capture, and wounded him for life. The foolish young seaman never thought for a moment of such a result. He probably lost his own life with his comrades. As for the Captain a grape shot pierced his knee, disabling him for life and compelling him to retire from active service.*

The *Patriot* and the *Tartar* continued to defend the Virginia coast from the British until the end of the war under Captain Barron, who died in 1787. Although Taylor was barely able to hobble around on crutches, the governor of Virginia and the Naval Board retained him as the virtual head of coastal defense with the rank of commodore until the close of hostilities.

In 1794, Taylor settled in Oldham County on a tract of 5,333 acres given to him for his service in the Revolutionary War. He brought his family, one hundred slaves and other personal property and livestock, settling close to Goshen off Buckeye and Shiloh Lanes. His property extended to the Ohio

River, but he built a two-story log home that sat back about a mile from the river, naming it Woodlawn.

Taylor was friends with General Marquis de LaFayette, and when LaFayette made his visit to America as a guest of the nation in 1824, he visited the commodore and his family. Taylor's granddaughter, who lived at Woodlawn until she was fourteen years old at the time of Taylor's death, recalled LaFayette sitting her on his lap and giving her a kiss, which caused her to be the envy of all her playmates. A few years before LaFayette's visit to Woodlawn, the little girl's mother, Matilda Taylor, had a beautiful family wedding at Woodlawn in May 1799 that was known as the event of the year. Matilda married her childhood sweetheart, Isaac Robertson. They met in Virginia before the Taylor family moved to Oldham County. Isaac became an attorney and studied law under Bushrod Washington in Richmond, Virginia.

By 1810, the Robertson family had settled in Frankfort, where Isaac practiced law before the court of appeals. The Robertsons had several children during this time and boarded at a local hotel in Frankfort. One tragic afternoon, Robertson had an altercation with portrait painter Samuel Dearborn about a room in the hotel. Dearborn slipped up behind Robertson and fatally stabbed him in the back while Robertson was playing on the hotel lawn with his children. Matilda took her children to Woodlawn and cared for her father and kept house for him after her mother's death.

In 1817, Congress approved and passed a measure for the relief of Commodore Taylor with an annual pension for as long as he lived. His great-grandson and namesake, Colonel Richard Taylor Jacob, was born at Woodlawn on March 14, 1825. Colonel Jacob had a beautiful monument of red granite erected over the graves of the commodore and his wife. The base of the granite slab contains the stones from the chimneys of Woodlawn. In 1959, the Peter Foree Chapter of the Daughters of the American Revolution officially marked the grave, which is located on private property on an Oldham County farm.

HERMITAGE FARM

Hermitage Farm was part of a land grant that was bought by Captain John Henshaw in Virginia in the early 1800s. He gave the land to his son, Phillip Telfair Henshaw, who married Sarah Ann Scott. They moved to Kentucky and began to build their home in 1832, and it was finished in 1835. They modeled their home after the Henshaw house in Orange County, Virginia.

The house is practically four stories tall because there is an attic and an English basement in which the dining room, kitchen, dairy, pantry, entry and two cellars are located. The front steps lead to a double-roofed porch ending in a gable in front of the middle of the attic. The second-story porch was often a sleeping porch when it was warm, and the first-floor porch literally became the sitting room of the family during the summer. The corners of the house were set on the cardinal points of the compass—the parlor in the north corner, the sitting room in the west, father's room in the south corner and a little room in the east corner so the front door faces directly northwest. The gateposts at the farm's main entrance and at several other gateways on the farm were quarried on the farm by slaves, entirely by hand. To cut the

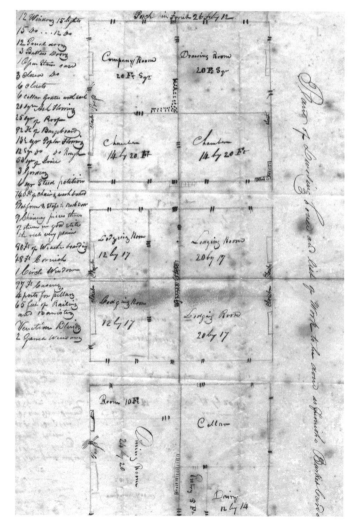

Original house plans drawn for Hermitage Farm for the Henshaw family.

gateposts, each weighing about two tons, the workers used a steel bar about one inch in thickness and sharpened at each end.

During construction of Hermitage, the Henshaws had returned to Virginia to visit family when Phillip got scarlet fever and died. Sarah Ann Scott Henshaw returned to the Hermitage a widow with their three small children, Sarah Ann Elizabeth, John Scott and Lucy Mary Jane.

Lucy Mary Jane married Richard Waters in the mid-1800s. Also living at the farm at that time was Sarah Ann Scott Henshaw; she lived there until her death in 1862. During this time, there were forty slaves who lived on the farm, including their weaver, Hannah, as well as George Page, who was central to many of the farm activities and successes therein. The Waterses had five children and gave Hermitage to one of their sons, Phillip Edmund Waters, who married twice and raised thirteen children on the farm. Phillip Edmund Waters is credited for bringing orchard grass to Kentucky, making

Hermitage farmhouse, photo taken in the 1920s.

Queen Elizabeth walks alongside Hermitage Farm owner Warner Jones in 1982.

Oldham County the leading orchard grass region in the nation. In 1936, the farm was sold to the Warner Jones family.

Under Warner and Harriet Jones, Hermitage became one of the most famous thoroughbred horse farms in the nation. Warner and Harriet raised their twin daughters at Hermitage. Warner Jones is the only person to breed winners of the Kentucky Derby (Dark Star), Kentucky Oaks (Nancy Jr.) and a Breeders' Cup race (Is It True). In addition, Jones broke the Keeneland yearling sales with a record sale of $13.1 million in 1985 for Seattle Dancer. In 1986, the queen of England visited Hermitage after meeting the Joneses through a mutual friend, Will Farrish, in Versailles. Warner Jones died at age seventy-eight in 1994. A longtime family friend, Carl Pollard, bought Hermitage Farm and continued the Hermitage tradition.

THE WESTPORT LIGHTHOUSE

A few years ago, in 2007, Oldham County resident Loren Johnson bought the property across the river from Westport, Kentucky, that contains the remnants of what is known as the "Westport Lighthouse." Loren shared photographs and the lighthouse history so that others could enjoy the benefit of the lighthouse's role on the edge of the Ohio River. The following is taken from notes that Johnson compiled regarding the site:

The old lighthouse is located on property originally called Bowyer's Landing. A ferry was operated there by Levi Bowyer as early as 1800 to form a link in the route to the Indiana territory. Levi's great-granddaughter said that Levi built a boat at Fort Washington (now Cincinnati) and floated it down to Westport. He unloaded his family, came back across the river to the Indiana side and drove a stake in the ground; then he walked to Vincennes, Indiana, to claim the land. It took him two weeks to walk there and back. He took the cabin off the flatboat that he had built and placed it on the Indiana property, making it a home for his family.

Bowyer operated a ferry that connected Westport to the Indiana territory, and it became a trade route for local citizens. The ferry was propelled by horsepower, and it took quite a while to make the river crossing. Mail was dropped off by flatboats coming down the river, and a horseback rider took the mail to New Washington, Indiana, for distribution. Farmers and businesses would come from the interior of Kentucky and Indiana to trade stock and goods across the two states. The stone foundation of the building was used as a general store, post office and saloon.

Westport Lighthouse, photo taken in 1970s. *Courtesy Loren Johnson.*

According to other Bowyer descendants, Levi Bowyer would bring women and children across the river on his ferry when there was danger of Indian raids. There he would stay on guard at the blockhouse. Levi was a member of the Militia Guards during the time of the Pigeon Roost Massacre in 1812. His name is on the roll spelled Levi "Boyer." Bowyer was a wheelwright by trade, and women used his spinning wheels to spin reels of wool and flax. Levi lived from 1773 to 1850.

After Bowyer's death, the property changed ownership over the ensuing years. In the 1930s, Mr. and Mrs. George Theodore Johnston bought the property, designing and building a home to resemble a lighthouse. The framework from the old river tavern was used in the new house, and the foundation from the tavern was used for the foundation of the new house and the stone wall below it. The bottom level of the house was a basement that included a brick furnace. The first level consisted of a living room, dining room and kitchen. The next level was reached by means of a winding exterior stairway in the rear of the house. The first dome was reached by climbing up and around the roof, and the top dome was reached from the first dome.

George "Theo" Johnston was a general contractor by trade and owned the Economy Paint Company at Campbell and Market in Louisville. He built numerous buildings locally, including homes, barns and a sternwheeler, the *Letitia W.*, for Dr. Watkins. Unfortunately, after completing their unusual "lighthouse" home, the 1937 flood hit, destroying much of the work and details that the Johnstons had so carefully executed.

In the winter, when the trees are bare, the old wagon tracks are still visible from aerial photographs as they progress down the steep slopes of Indiana to reach the Westport crossing. The old tracks and the stone foundation serve as a reminder of the time when Oldham County was a gateway for the pioneers as they moved westward to a new frontier.

EARLY COURTHOUSE DOCUMENTS

The Oldham County History Center archives hold county records that go back to the county's formation. The following quoted material is taken from those county records.

This trial is the first murder trial recorded in the circuit court books, and it describes the plight of an African American woman, Lucy, who was enslaved by Elizabeth Smith. Although one may never know the reason behind Lucy's motives, it is an insightful look regarding the feelings of those who were enslaved during this period of history. The document was written on May 18, 1825, and was an indictment of Lucy, a women of color, for the "poising" of Elizabeth Smith with pulverized glass on September 7, 1824.

> *States of Kentucky, Oldham County and current set.*
> *The grand jurors for the commonwealth of Kentucky empanelled, charged and sworn in the county of Oldham and state aforesaid, represented on choirs oaths that Lucy a female slave of colour the property of Isaac Smith of Oldham county being a person of wicked mind and disposition and*

Original court document of the first murder trial, concerning "Lucy, Woman of Color," in Oldham County.

maliciously, intending to poison one Elizabeth Smith did on the seventh day of September in the year of our lord one thousand eight hundred and twenty four in the county of aforesaid willingly maliciously and feloniously disguised a large quantity of pulverized glafs, being a deadly poison, into a vessel filled with water, which water the said Elizabeth had then and there immediately before directed the said Lucy to boil in order to make a certain diet or liquor called soup for her own drink or consumption, and the said Lucy did then and there willfully maliciously and feloniously boiled the said pulverized glafs in the said water, and did immediately afterwards vomit on the day and year aforesaid delivered the said water made into soup with the said large quantity of glafs pulverized as aforesaid mixed therein to the said Elizabeth Smith to use as a diet or drink and the said Elizabeth Smith not knowing the said pulverized glass to have been in the said soup, did use the same as diet or drink, whereby the said Elizabeth Smith became grievously and violently distempered—in consequences thereof did pine away and die on the seventh day of September in the year of our lord one thousand eight hundred and twenty four[.] And the grand jurors aforesaid upon there oath aforesaid do say that the said Lucy did feloniously willfully and maliciously administered the poison to the said Elizabeth whereof she died a gavel the form of the statute in such cases made and provided and against the peace and dignity of the commonwealth of Kentucky.

And the grand jurors aforesaid on there oaths do further present that the aforesaid Lucy a female slave of colour the property of Isaac Smith being instigated by the civil, maliciously intending to poison the aforesaid Elizabeth Smith did on the twentieth day of September the year of our lord one thousand and eight hundred and twenty four in the county aforesaid willfully, maliciously and feloniously disguised a large quantity of pulverized glafs in a certain vessel filled with water which water she the said Elizabeth had then and there immediately before directed the said Lucy to boil in order to make a certain drink or diet called soup for she the said Elizabeth to drink or consume and the said Lucy did then and there intending the said Elizabeth to poison willfully maliciously and feloniously boil the said pulverized glafs in said water and did immediately afterwards on the seventh day of September in the year aforesaid in the county aforesaid delivered the said water made into soup as aforesaid with the said pulverized glafs disguised therein to the said Elizabeth smith and the said Elizabeth not knowing or suspecting the said pulverized glafs to be or to have been in said soup did use a large quantity of the said soup with much of the said pulverized glafs disguised therein as aforesaid shortly after which the said

*Elizabeth was grievously afflicted and did pine and died against the form
of the statue in such cases made and provided and against the peace and
dignity of the commonwealth of Kentucky summon.*

Wm J. Graves attorney

For the commonwealth

Provided

Court records indicated that Lucy was indicted for murder and
sentenced accordingly (in those years it would have been death by
hanging). There are no records of her execution.

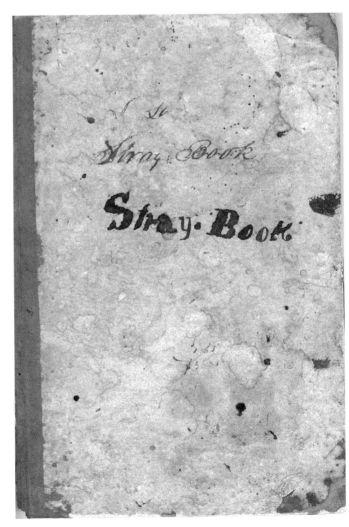

The Stray Book
is an example of
an early court
document. It
was used to
record wandering
livestock that
could be claimed
by a finder, if
approved through
court action.

LaGrange City Minutes

LaGrange operated under a board of trustees that was formed on March 11, 1848. The town was not large enough to qualify for city status under state law. In fact, the city was not incorporated as such with an official mayor until 1910. The following are minutes transcribed from the Oldham County History Archives records of the City of LaGrange Minutes, 1848–76. In this series, John Keynon was the chairman of the board of trustees. Keynon was proprietor of the Keynon Hotel, located on Main Street (now occupied in the same place by the LaGrange Fire & Rescue Deptartment).

Daily, Weekly, and Dollar Weekly Louisville Democrat.

HARNEY, HUGHES & CO., Proprietors.

305 and 307 Third Street, between Market and Jefferson.

Louisville, Ky., Aug 9th 1862

James Maunt Esq

Dear Sir

Enclosed please find bill as per your request, which amount please remit at your convenience and oblige.

Yours &c

Harney Hughes & Co

Fonda

Notice.

ON THE 2D DAY OF JULY, 1862, A NEGRO Man calling himself GEORGE was committed to the Oldham county jail as a runaway slave. He is about 30 years old, 5 feet and 5 inches old, copper color, and lame in the left thigh; is rather intelligent, and says he belongs to Baker Ewing, of Owen county, Ky. The Owner can come forward, prove property and pay charges, or said negro man man will be dealt with as the law requires.

JAMES MAUNT, J. O. C.

LaGrange, Ky., July 31st, 1862.   au1 d&wtf

NOTICE.

ON THE 23D DAY OF JULY, 1862, A NEGRO Woman calling herself MARY, and a boy-child about two years old, were committed to the Oldham County jail as runaway slaves. Said Woman is very black, four feet ten inches high, and is about 22 years old; says she and the child belong to Morgan Perry, of Owen county, Kentucky. The owner can come forward, prove property and pay charges, else, said negroes will be dealt with as the law requires.

JAMES MAUNT, J. O. C.

LaGrange, Ky., July 31st, 1862.   au1 d&wtf

Runaway slave advertisements that were posted by LaGrange town marshal James Mount in a Louisville newspaper.

LaGrange, Dec. 5, 1853

Trustees met at Mr. Keynon's.

Present: John Keynon, Brent Hopkins, Samuel Grimes, W.W. Hosclaw, James Hopwood, and G.W .Ray.

Mr. C.A. Frederic declined the office of clerk and Thos. S. Wells appointed in his place.

The Board then proceeded to levy a tax for 1852 fixing the same at 10 cents on the $1.00 and 50 cents pole tax. The order to assess the town property for 1853 was received. On motion Samuel Grimes is ordered to repair the street running from the Reform Church to the Eastern boundary of the town so as not to expend more than $20 and report to the Board.

On motion, Brent Hopkins, Samuel Grimes and G.W. Ray are appointed a committee to revise the town ordinances. On motion, it is ordered that the Town Marshal notify all the citizens living on Main and Main Cross Streets, also Madison Street corner of Wm. Hopkins lot to Wm. Fitzgerald, to remove all obstructions from said streets, and that the Marshal have them clear in 10 days from this date. Also the alleys back of Mr. Keynon and Kightleys alley to be cleared out.

It is also ordered that the Marshal have the bridge and mud hole near the Depot repaired and report the cost to this Board.

Resolved that the regular meetings of this Board shall be holden [sic] on the 1st and 3rd Monday evenings of each month. Adjoined to Monday evening next

Test.

Thomas Wells, Clerk   John Keynon, Chm.

LaGrange, May 8, 1855

Trustees met

Present: J. Keynon, W.W. Morlan, J. Hopwood and Samuel Grimes

On motion a charge of $3.00 is entered against T.G. Barfiel, improperly allowed him 6th Feb 54 which amount was due to W.J. Keynon for lumber furnished for bridge. J. Keynon has received $1 amount in past payment of his tax.

On motion Mr. J. Keynon is allowed $2.00 for furnishing room to date.

The town Marshal is requested to deliver notices to the Superintendent and Capt. Kears not to run his train so rapidly through the town of LaGrange.

The town Marshal is also instructed to prevent marble playing in the town limits on Sundays.

The town assessor is ordered to list the town property and make return of said list by 1ˢᵗ of June next.

The board then adjourned to meet on Saturday night next

John Keynon, Chm.

LaGrange, May 26ᵗʰ, 1855

Trustees met

Present: J. Keynon, B. Hopkins, J.M. Leggett and W.W. Morlaw.

Mr. A.M. Garlay offered his bonds as town Treasurer with Mr. John Keynon security, bond received and clerk ordered to file the same.

Mr. James Mount also offered his bonds as town Marshal and Collector with Mr. E.F. Waide security same received and ordered filed.

On motion it is ordered that the Marshal act as town patrol and that he take due notice of all slaves visiting the town of LaGrange at church or otherwise on Sunday, without papers, after first giving them notice.

On motion, it is ordered, that the town Marshal shall receive the same fees as constables for similar services.

On motion the Board adjourned.

John Keynon, Chm.

As tension began to mount over the issues of slavery, abolition and volatile rumors of states seceding from the Union, the LaGrange Board of Trustees began to issue more ordinances regarding control of the slaves as fugitive slaves began to be more of an issue.

May 26, 1855

On motion it is ordered that the Marshall act as town patrol, and that he take due notice of all slaves visiting the town of LaGrange at church or otherwise on Sunday without papers, after first giving them notice.

May 1, 1861

Trustees met

On motion of Mr. W.C. Mahan was appointed to ring the court house bell every night at nine o'clock. Also to notify slave and slave holders, the object of said ringing, and after 10 days from the adoption of said motion, slaves caught from home, and liable to be whipped by the town Marshal or Patrol.

June 12, 1861

Call Meeting

On motion. W.C. Mahan was allowed five dollars for ringing of 9 o'clock bell up to date.

There being no further business the Board adjourned.

July 20, 1863

On motion. It is ordered that the town clerk post up notices in the town of LaGrange that owners of slaves shall not give their slaves papers to pass or repass in the town of LaGrange after the hour of 9 o'clock p.m. and any slaves found in said town after said hour are to be reported to the town Marshall.

August 17, 1863

By law offered. Inflicting a penalty upon slaves guilty of running horses through the streets of said town or using obscene language on the streets in the hearing of white persons.

SLAVERY AT RIVER'S EDGE

Kentucky was one of the northernmost slave states but never seceded from the Union during the Civil War. According to Lewis and Richard Collins, records indicate that the population of Oldham County included 4,815 whites and 2,431 slaves in 1860 prior to the onset of the Civil War. Most of the slaves came with the English families from Virginia after the Revolutionary War. The slave trade in Oldham County prospered, particularly after Congress passed an act in 1808 that prohibited slave trade from outside of the United States. People traded and sold slaves within the United States borders, often making large sums of money. The Ohio River became an important corridor for slave trafficking and formed a part of the Underground Railroad for slaves who chose to runaway. The following explores some of the relationships of slave owners and enslaved persons at the river's edge.

Henry Bibb and William Gatewood

The years leading to the Civil War were full of unrest and tension over the issues of economics and slavery. Abraham Lincoln's stance on slavery shifted during the course of his career leading to his presidency. Lincoln was very sensitive to Kentucky's proslavery stance and felt that support from border states such as Kentucky was a key factor to keep the nation from a civil war. It was a refugee slave from Kentucky, Henry Bibb (1814–1854), who played an important role in the abolitionist movement leading up to the Civil War.

As a young boy, Bibb was the playmate of slave owners' children, and he mastered the English language and became a prolific writer. He fell in love with a slave from Oldham County named Malinda, and they produced a daughter, Francis. William Gatewood, who enslaved Bibb and his family, sold the Bibb family after frustration with Bibb's repeated attempts to escape. Eventually, through a series of other slave owners, Bibb was separated from Malinda and Francis and escaped to the free states to help with the antislavery movement. From his experiences as a slave, Bibb wrote his slave narratives and published them in 1849. The narratives were used to raise funds to establish land in Canada for refugee slaves. The following correspondence took place between Henry Bibb and William Gatewood after Gatewood had received a pamphlet concerning Bibb's abolitionist activities.

THE first direct information that I received concerning any of my relations, after my last escape from slavery, was communicated in a letter from Wm. H. Gatewood, my former owner, which I here insert word for word, without any correction:

"BEDFORD, TRIMBLE COUNTY, KY.

Mr. H. BIBB.

DEAR SIR:—After my respects to you and yours &c., I received a small book which you sent to me that I peroseed and found it was sent by H. Bibb I am a stranger in Detroit and know no man there without it is Walton H. Bibb if this be the man please to write to me and tell me all about that place and the people I will tell you the news here as well as I can your mother is still living here and she is well the people are generally well in this country times are dull and produce low give my compliments to King, Jack, and all my friends in that cuntry I read that book you sent me and think it will do very well—George is sold, I do not know any thing about him I have nothing more at present, but remain yours &c
W.H. GATEWOOD.
February 9th, 1844.
P.S. You will please to answer this letter."

Never was I more surprised than at the reception of this letter, it came so unexpected to me. There had just been a State Convention held in Detroit, by the free people of color, the proceedings of which were published in pamphlet form. I forwarded several of them to distinguished slaveholders in Kentucky—one among others was Mr. Gatewood, and gave him to understand who sent it. After showing this letter to several of my anti-slavery friends, and asking their opinions about the propriety of my answering it, I was advised to do it, as Mr. Gatewood had no claim on me as a slave, for he had sold and got the money for me and my family. So I wrote him an answer, as near as I can recollect, in the following language:

"Detroit, March 23*d*, 1844.
William Gatewood

DEAR SIR:—*I am happy to inform you that you are not mistaken in the man whom you sold as property, and received pay for as such. But I thank God that I am not property now, but am regarded as a man like yourself, and although I live far north, I am enjoying a comfortable living by my own industry. If you should ever chance to be traveling this way, and will call on me, I will use you better than you did me while you held me as a slave. Think not that I have any malice against you, for the cruel treatment which you inflicted on me while I was in your power. As it was the custom of your country, to treat your fellow men as you did me and my little family, I can freely forgive you.*

I wish to be remembered in love to my aged mother, and friends; please tell her that if we should never meet again in this life, my prayer shall be to God that we may meet in Heaven, where parting shall be no more.

You wish to be remembered to King and Jack. I am pleased, sir, to inform you that they are both here, well, and doing well. They are both living in Canada West. They are now the owners of better farms than the men are who once owned them.

You may perhaps think hard of us for running away from slavery, but as to myself, I have but one apology to make for it, which is this: I have only to regret that I did not start at an earlier period. I might have been free long before I was. But you had it in your power to have kept me there much longer than you did. I think it is very probable that I should have been a toiling slave on your plantation to-day, if you had treated me differently. To be compelled to stand by and see you whip and slash my wife without mercy, when I could afford her no protection, not

even by offering myself to suffer the lash in her place, was more than I felt it to be the duty of a slave husband to endure, while the way was open to Canada. My infant child was also frequently flogged by Mrs. Gatewood, for crying, until its skin was bruised literally purple. This kind of treatment was what drove me from home and family, to seek a better home for them. But I am willing to forget the past. I should be Pleased to hear from you again, on the reception of this, and should also be very happy to correspond with you often, if it should be agreeable to yourself. I subscribe myself a friend to the oppressed, and Liberty forever.
HENRY BIBB. "

In 1848, Bibb appeared before the circuit court of the U.S. district of Michigan to denounce the institution of slavery. He became actively associated with the Liberty Party in Michigan and was the chairman pro tem for the North American Convention of Colored People in 1851. Although there is no record that shows where Bibb and Lincoln met, Lincoln was very interested in the ideas of the separatist movement. The movement called for the relocation of slaves to another country. There were four leading figures who advocated separatism during the 1840s and '50s. Bishop James Holly advocated separatism for Haiti, Martin Delaney for South America, Henry Highland Garnett for Africa and Henry Bibb for Canada.

Bibb favored refugees to colonize in Canada. Unlike Frederick Douglass, who felt that slaves should immediately become freed citizens of the United States, Bibb felt that there needed to be a period of adjustment during which slaves could be educated and build their own community. Canada provided a close haven from which refugees from slavery could one day return to their homeland in the United States.

Lincoln was aware of the exodus of slaves to Canada, particularly after the Compromise of 1850 that strengthened the Slave Fugitive Act. It was Henry Bibb who raised funds to buy land in Canada, and Bibb established a community of refugees that he named the Refugee's Home Colony. The *Voice of the Fugitive* became the title of a newspaper that Bibb created and edited in Canada.

In 2004, the Oldham County History Center initiated an archaeological program at the old Gatewood Plantation, outside of Bedford, Kentucky, to explore the antebellum home of William Gatewood, who enslaved Bibb and his family. Many volunteers have helped excavate the site, as

Remains of the William Gatewood farmhouse where Henry Bibb and his wife lived as slaves. The site is currently under archaeological investigation, conducted by the Oldham County History Center..

well as research the records and places that Bibb mentioned in his slave narratives. From the archival records, William Gatewood has emerged in several instances.

Gatewood was justice of the peace in Oldham County and served warrants issued by the circuit court. Gatewood was indicted by the circuit court for hiring out one of his slaves, Mahala. It is assumed that he hired her out for prostitution and more than likely collected fees for her services.

THE MOUNT FAMILY

James and Amanda Mount lived in LaGrange, Kentucky, in the mid- to late 1800s and were active in small-town business and community affairs. Amanda Mount was the great-niece of Elizabeth Railey, who was Thomas Jefferson's mother. In 2002, a widow of a Mount descendant presented a box to the Oldham County History Center that contained Mount family documents and history. Known as Grandma Railey's box, the documents contained slave ownership papers, slave bounty receipts and Civil War letters written to Amanda by her nephew, Amos, who served in the Union army. The following is an excerpt of a letter written by J.J. Railey, Amanda's brother, to James and Amanda regarding the sale of some of their slaves.

> *Louisville, April 13, 1852*
> *Dear Sir:*
>
> *I read your letter for Will Keynon on last Saturday and was very much astonished to hear you and Sister Amanda was opposed to my selling Anarchy and child for $400 where you both had told me to sell her for the best price I could get and that you all would be satisfied, that I was to sell for Mother Anarchy and her two children for the best price I could get, and that the money was then to be equally divided between you, James and myself. This was agreed by you and James, so that mother could effect a sale without obtaining a decree of court, thereby saving a great expense and that you wanted George and would pay or take him at one hundred and seventy five dollars. I told you I was willing for you to have him at that price provided James was willing. And I want you to write me word if you still want him at that price for if you do not, I can get more for him, either here or in LaGrange. I think strange you all should object now to my selling Anarchy and children for $400—after telling me to do the best I could and you would be satisfied, and seemed to be willing for Dr. Yocum to have her for $200—now if the bill of sale had been made and sent down to me as I discussed—I had sold her and children for $400, as is did not come I missed the sale and don't know when I can sell her again.*
> *Yours truly,*
> *J.J. Railey*

When President Lincoln issued the Emancipation Proclamation in January 1863, all slaves in the Confederacy were legally free, but this did not apply to Kentucky because Kentucky had declared for the Union. In 1864, Lincoln declared that any slave who enlisted for the Union would be given freedom, as well as freedom for his family. A flood of Kentucky slaves rushed to enlist at Camp Nelson. The following are two receipts for Amanda Mount from bounty hunters who had captured slaves who had enlisted. There were over twenty-five thousand colored troops who enlisted from Kentucky and fought for the Union. African American soldiers supplied almost one-fourth of the total Union forces furnished by Kentucky. The following receipts ignore Lincoln's declaration of freed black soldiers.

1864 Jas. Mount

To Wm. S. Bennett

To trouble, expense aside on taking runaway negro soldier to Louisville from
   LaGrange, collecting money for $15.70.

Rec. Nov. 21, 1864 of A.R. Mount adv of Jas Mount due the amount
   in full, under my hand.

W.S. Bennett

In another receipt:

Received of Mrs. Am. R. Mount her claim for two slaves who are supposed
to be in the service of the United States government.

May the date 1864

J.W. Cardwell & Co. per J.P. Sharp

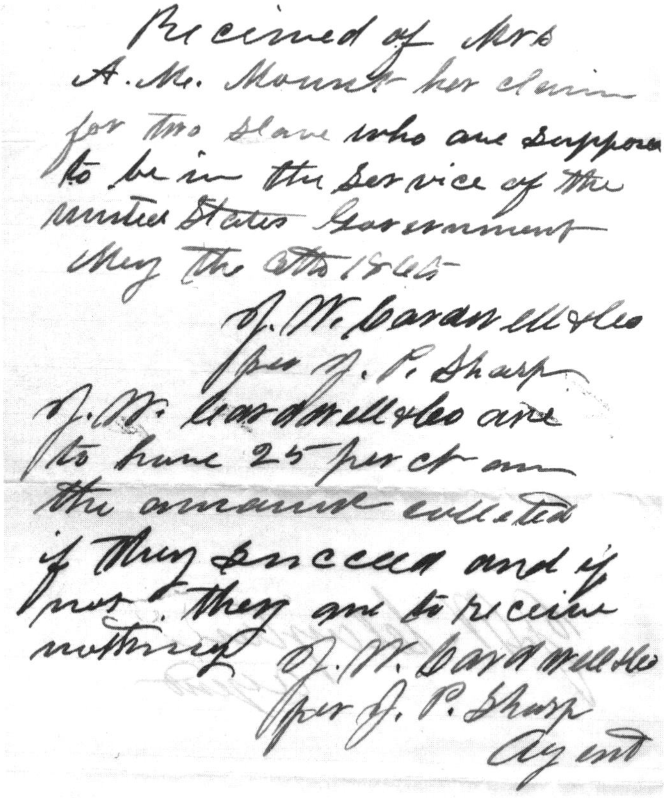

A bounty hunter contract for runaway slaves, issued by Amanda Mount, who was Amos Mount's aunt.

Mrs. Amanda Mount (middle) sits on the front porch of her home surrounded by her daughter-in-law and granddaughters. The Mount home has been restored and is now the location for the archives for the Oldham County Historical Society.

J. W. Cardwell & Co. are to have 25 perct of the amount collected if they succeed and if not they are to receive nothing.
J. W. Cardwell & Co. per J.P. Sharp, Agent

JAMES STAPLETON CRUTCHFIELD

James Crutchfield was born in 1800 on a farm near Goshen. His father died when James was ten, and he moved in with the Duerson family, who lived nearby. His cousin was Zachary Taylor, who was later elected president of the United States. Crutchfield was known as a generous, honest and fair man and was a freemason and member of the local fortitude lodge that began in Westport and later moved to LaGrange. Crutchfield was appointed Oldham County's first sheriff by the governor of Kentucky in 1823 and served as such for eight years. Historian Lucien Rule writes in 1922 of Crutchfield:

Mr. Crutchfield was an absolutely fearless man as sheriff of the county. Out in the Patten Creek hills there lived a desperate character with the

Sheriff James Crutchfield was well liked and known for his fair and honest approach when dealing with controversial situations.

reputation of bluffing every officer of the law who ever tackled him. He said he would shoot a sheriff or deputy at sight. Mr. Crutchfield was sheriff eight years, and one morning rode out to make a levy on the man. The backwoodsman came to the fence with his rifle in his hand. The sheriff dismounted, threw his bridle rein over a rail, stepped over the fence, advancing to meet the man with clear fearless eyes. "Now," said he, "I am here to serve notice on you; if you will act with sense then I can help you; but if you resist there will be trouble!" The man gave in, and afterward became the best friend the sheriff had in the community.

Mr. Crutchfield was an expert river man. He spent sometime in Louisiana aboard a boat in Red River, where his brother had interests. He was a good pilot, taking his brother's place when he died and selling the boat for his estate years afterward. Whenever Mr. Crutchfield went to Louisville he would go up into the pilot house and take his place at the wheel. He would ride all day as sheriff and then ship cord wood from his farm to Louisville. There was a woodchopper working for him who was a giant. He was seven feet tall, used a seven pound ax and could cut seven cords of wood per day. His great passion was liquor. One day he came to the farm house crazy drunk and wanted to kill the family with his ax. The whites and negroes were all in terror. Fortunately, Mr. Crutchfield was at hand. He went out in the back yard where the big Goliath was, ready to kill the first person in sight. Calling to a negro teamster, Mr. Crutchfield said, "Get the ox team and log chain and drag this drunken demon to the Ohio River! Be quick about it!" The big fellow staggered off in a hurry and was seen no more.

Another time there was a poor negro woman slave imprisoned on the charge of having poisoned her husband who seems to have died suddenly and mysteriously. The woman was condemned to die also, and her piteous moans moved Mr. Crutchfield so deeply that he began to doubt her case. An examination of the prisoner by the matron showed marks of brutal treatment on the poor woman's body. She broke down and protested her innocence to the matron and sheriff. He knew the character of the overseer on the farm from which she had been brought, and was strongly persuaded in his own mind that the negro husband had come to his end at the hands of the criminal overseer himself.

It was hardly possible to recall the miscarriage of justice now, since the trial was over and the woman was to die on the gallows. The confession was evidently extorted from her or force upon her by the lash of the overseer to shield himself. No slave could have a life sentence then, as death or the Southern field was the penalty.

But Mr. Crutchfield saddled his speediest horse, rode to Frankfort, saw the Governor, put the case before him and was soon back in LaGrange with a pardon for the poor woman. He was a Henry Clay emancipationist anyhow and his compassion for the negro toilers was proverbial. He was defeated upon that very issue as a candidate for delegate from his county—Oldham—to the constitutional convention of 1850, where the last attempt was made to abolish slavery by peaceful legislation, as Father David Rice, the grand old Presbyterian pioneer, had counseled and urged fifty years before as a member of the first constitutional convention, but was defeated also. Nevertheless, as a member of the Legislature, Mr. Crutchfield's voice was ever raised in behalf of freedom and humanity.

Crutchfield was such a great humanitarian and could not bear to execute a prisoner. He once gave a bystander $20 to act as deputy in his place for such a gruesome task when a man was to be hanged. It was also said that Crutchfield had a remarkable mind and memory. He purchased all the hogs of the community for shipment to the pork houses in Louisville. One day he weighed a lot of hogs for a farmer while Owen MaGruder kept the weights. One hog had to be weighed at a time. The job was almost done when Mr. Crutchfield said: "Owen, let me call off the weight of each hog to see if you have that column of figures correct." They were right, and Mr. Crutchfield made the calculations all mentally. He became a member of the

Goshen Presbyterian Church in the last years of his life and died mourned by as large a circle of friends and grateful people as ever followed a citizen of Oldham County to the tomb.

RECOLLECTIONS OF DR. STANTON PIERCE BRYAN AND HIS WIFE, ADELAIDE

Stanton Pierce Bryan was born in 1827, the son of Dr. Edmund and Lettie Pierce Bryan, and had fourteen siblings. Three of the fifteen children followed their father's profession and became medical doctors, Bryan being one of them. At twenty-two, Dr. Stanton left his family home in Wayne County and traveled to Louisville in hopes of entering medical school by earning money for his tuition teaching at a country school. He found a job in Oldhamsburg (now Skylight) for a summer term, and there he met a student who would become his future wife, Adelaide Thomas. He was admitted to medical school for the season of 1851–52 and received his degree in medicine. He and Adelaide Thomas were married in 1853.

In January 1854, Bryan took over the practice of Dr. Kellar in Brownsboro and was the practicing physician there for the next forty years. The following are some excerpts from diaries and stories from the Bryans' experiences in Oldham County that were compiled by his granddaughter, Adelaide Bostick.

On one dark night, Dr. Bryan was trying to reach a place somewhere near Buckner. He was riding, he thought, on the right trail when suddenly his horse stopped short and no amount of urging would induce him to take another step. There was nothing to do but to give him the reins. The animal immediately turned in the opposite direction, and finally their destination was reached. Next morning, the doctor went over the same ground and found that he had ridden to the very verge of a point where another step would have precipitated both horse and rider to probable destruction.

The lack of dentists also expanded Bryan's practice into dentistry and he took a special course in dentistry and fitted his office with full dental equipment. One of the doctor's favorite stories was about a slow-spoken, old gentleman who announced to the doctor: "Doc, you know I'm a pore [sic] man and we can't afford a mouthful of gold plugs like some; but I'm willing to do my part by my family, and I've told my three girls they can have one apiece."

To further his education, Bryan took a trip to Europe for six months to attend lectures and clinics at a number of different hospitals from November

Above, left: Dr. Stanton Bryan, pioneer physician in Brownsboro.

Above, right: Mrs. Adelaide Bryan, wife of Dr. Bryan, was known as a caring and gracious neighbor.

1856 to May 1857. The following are some letters written by wife, Adelaide to her husband in Europe about news from Brownsboro:

"*Feb. 21, 1857*

[excerpt] *Mrs. James Allen is sick, has the chills. They have not called a physician. Mrs. Allen says she wishes very much you were here and said I must tell you to come as quick as possible for her benefit. Feb. 22…*[continuation of same letter] *Josie has been right sick all day—has a severe cough, pain in her breast and side. I put a mustard plaster on her breast and have been giving her some cough drops you left. I have given her enough cough drops to vomit her and she has breathed easier since. I did not go to church today. Brother went. Cousin John Milton and his little girl took dinner with us and little Fannie had a chill. So you see we need you at home badly, yes very badly. Feb. 24th…*[same letter] *We are alone tonight. Brother (went to Westport) and has not gotten home and it is too dark and rainy to send for Mr. Caldwell. I am a little afraid to stay here without some gentleman in the house. However, I will try to be brave and not think of fear…Lou Carroway is very sick.*

Dr. James says she has Winter Fever. Cousin John Milton thinks she has pneumonia, and is talking about sending for some other physician—he is wishing very much you were here.

March 23rd...Tuesday evening I went up to Mrs.Bottorff's on the omnibus and a rough ride we had. Bettie [infant daughter] *was afraid of the cars and seemed badly frightened when they whistled. I have been gardening today, planted peas, radishes and lettuce and set my onions. Mr. Barrackman has promised to plant my Irish potatoes tomorrow. He broke up my garden while I was in Indiana.*

Dr. Rob Morris:
Poet Laureate, Freemason and Organizer of the Order of the Eastern Star

Dr. Rob Morris was born near Boston, Massachusetts, on August 31, 1818. He spent his early childhood and was educated in New York City. He received degrees in law and philosophy, was very interested in theology and devoted much of his time to Bible study. Dr. Morris moved south and became president of the DeSoto Academy, where he met Charlotte Mendenall, whom he married in 1841. They had nine children: John, Charlotte, Alfred, Robert, Sarah, Ruth, Electa, Ella and a child who died at birth.

Morris was inducted as a Freemason at the Gathright Lodge No. 33 in Oxford, Mississippi, on March 5, 1846. He began traveling to many cities in Mississippi and Tennessee, lecturing on Masonic history. Many of his poems, sermons and Masonic writings were composed during these travels. He also became very interested in reviving the Order of the Eastern Star, a Masonic organization for women.

In 1860, Dr. Morris was appointed professor of ancient and modern history at the Masonic College in LaGrange (also known as Funk Seminary) and moved his family to LaGrange. During that same year, Morris recalls a meeting he had with Abraham Lincoln:

In the month of October, 1860, about a month before the Presidential election of that year, we were in attendance upon the Grand Lodge of Illinois at Springfield, and in accordance with an invitation to that effect, called upon Mr. Lincoln.

As we were known to be no politician, but had written a severe article the month before denouncing the treasonable indications of Southern politics,

Dr. Rob Morris was poet laureate for Freemasonry in the nineteenth century. He helped to reorganize the Eastern Star for women and make it one of the largest charitable groups for women worldwide.

Mr. Lincoln was exceedingly courteous to us and gave us a lengthy and most pleasing conference.

To draw out of him in a pleasant manner the fact as to whether he was a Freemason or not, we remarked: "Mr. Lincoln, I came up the road last night with an old Masonic friend, Judge Douglas. Last Friday I came down to Louisville with another old Masonic friend, Mr. Breckinridge. And a few weeks ago one of my agents, Mr. Porter, met in the Grand Lodge of Tennessee, Mr. John Bell. So you see all three of your opponents for the Presidential chair are Freemasons!"

Mr. Lincoln replied: "I am not a Freemason, Dr. Morris, though I have a great respect for the institution."

Muddy Waters

In September 1861, Dr. Morris accepted a commission as a Masonic lecturer under the grand master of Indiana. Because of his commission, and Morris's outspoken stance against the South, he soon paid the price of his loyalty to the Union, according to Lucien Rule:

> *It was upon this tour while at Crowne Point, Indiana, November 7th, that my dwelling at LaGrange was burned by the midnight torch and my family turned out to the night air homeless. By the great good fortune of a camp of Federal soldiers being hard by, my costly collections of Masonic books were saved, though in a mangled condition. I received the intelligence next day by telegraph and hastened home to comfort the distressed group.*
>
> *Early in September of this year the prospects of the subjugation of Kentucky by the Confederate armies appeared to me so imminent that I withdrew my membership from Fortitude Lodge No. 47, LaGrange, of which I had become a member the year before and was now the master, and prepared to move my family to New York. The intention, however, was changed shortly after as the danger alluded to passed away.*

Rob Morris was anointed the poet laureate of Freemasonry for the nineteenth century in 1884. The only other person to receive such distinction was Scottish poet Robert Burns, who took the honor as poet laureate of Freemasonry for the eighteenth century. He also traveled many places, including two trips to the Middle East, where he started a Freemasonry chapter. The Rob Morris Home is now a historic museum owned by the Order of the Eastern Star. It is located on the corner of Washington and Cedar Streets in LaGrange.

The following is an excerpt of Morris's most popular poem, "The Level and The Square"; written in August 1854, it had fifteen musical compositions set to it as song or declamation and has made the rounds of the Masonic world:

The Level and the Square

We meet upon the Level and we part upon the Square:
What words of precious meaning those words Masonic are!
Come, let us contemplate them! They are worthy of a thought;
In the very walls of Masonry the sentiment is wrought.
We meet upon the Level, though from every station come,
The rich man from his palace and the poor man from his home;

For the rich must leave his wealth and state outside the Mason's door,
And the poor man finds his best respect upon the Checkered floor.

There's a World where all are equal, we are hurrying towards it fast,
We shall meet upon the Level there, when the gates of Death are passed;
We shall stand before the Orient, and our Master will be there,
To try the blocks we offer with His own unerring Square.

Hands round, ye faithful Brotherhood, the bright fraternal chain,
We part upon the Square below, to meet in Heaven again!
What words of precious meaning those words Masonic are,—
We meet upon the Level and we part upon the Square.

THE MASONIC UNIVERSITY OF KENTUCKY: FUNK SEMINARY

William M. Funk died at age twenty-seven on September 18, 1841, and left $10,000 to establish a seminary in his name to be run by the Grand Lodge of Kentucky as the only college ever organized by a secret order in the United States. His last will and testament states: "I wish the sum of ten thousand dollars appropriated to the establishment of an institution of learning in LaGrange to be called Funk Seminary provided the citizens of Oldham County subscribe and pay the sum of $5,000 in aid of said institution."

By an act of legislature on February 22, 1842, Funk Seminary was incorporated. The site chosen was composed of four lots behind the public square in LaGrange and cost $350. The building was completed in 1843 and described as a substantial and commodious college edifice, measuring fifty by sixty-five feet, two stories high with eight rooms. The brick building cost $4,500 to build, and its edifice was supported by a pediment gable, supported by four large columns, forming a vestibule. The school was managed by the Grand Lodge to be established "and endowed at the expense of the Grand Lodge and at which they might educate the orphans of Masonry on the labor principle by teaching them to practice healthy labor and mechanical arts in addition to the useful branches and English education."

Early twentieth-century reporter W.C. Barrickman wrote that, during one of the Christmas holidays during the school's earlier years, students decided that the "pedimented" gable was not adequately ornamental, so they "borrowed" in front of Sauer's store on Main Street a nice red farm

Funk Seminary, established in 1842, served as a orphanage, then became a college and lastly served as a elementary school and high school until it burned down in 1911.

wagon, took it apart and carefully and laboriously reassembled it astride the building's ridge top!

The first session of the school opened on the first Monday of November 1844, with a primary department for "reading, writing, 'orthography,' arithmetic, geography and grammar." In the senior department, the course of study was "Science, literature, Latin and Greek," with French and Spanish extra. Citizens of LaGrange and Oldham County would be permitted to send their sons as "pay students" with annual tuition being six dollars for primary students and ten dollars for higher department.

By 1848, a female school at LaGrange had also voluntarily come under Grand Lodge control, total enrollment was in excess of 170 students (including charity students from twelve lodges) and the name had changed to the Masonic Seminary and Masonic College. Through the diligent efforts of the Grand Lodge of Kentucky, the state legislature in 1850 deemed it appropriate to confer upon the college the full rights and privileges of a university. It was at this time that the name was changed to the Masonic University of Kentucky, and the Grand Lodge of Kentucky appropriated $1,000 for the education of female children of deceased master Masons.

During the period of 1850 to 1861, the university made decided headway and progress, growing to full reenrollment and enjoying a reputation for sound scholarship. The school boasted that there were students from Kentucky, Missouri, Tennessee, Mississippi and Louisiana. This came to a sudden end in 1861 with the outbreak of the Civil War. The student body quickly disintegrated over the Civil War years, and the faculty gradually dissolved. The strain of the Reconstruction period drained the essential funding needed from the Grand Lodge. On May 1, 1873, the Masonic University of Kentucky ceased to exist, and the Grand Lodge returned the property and school equipment to the trustees, according to the will and testament of William Funk.

The school returned to a high school status and continued to operate as Funk Seminary, LaGrange High School, until the building burned down on the night of September 24, 1911. Rumors had it that the fire was accidentally set by gamblers who were said to have used the cupola of the building for "surreptitious" games.

The modern Oldham County Fiscal Court building was modeled to resemble the Old Funk Seminary and occupies the same area. There is a historic marker beside the building that identifies the Funk Seminary site.

Part II

TURBULENCE

With the advent of the railroad in 1854, LaGrange became the major seat of county activities. The Union troops utilized the railroad to their advantage and could transport troops easier and faster than the Confederacy. The southwestern area of the county seemed to be more sympathetic to the Confederacy, while those in the northeastern areas were more sympathetic to the Union cause. The sentiments for the Confederacy were so strong in Crestwood and the Pewee Valley area that after the Civil War it became a location for a statewide retirement home for Confederate veterans with a special burial ground established nearby.

During the period of Reconstruction, the romantic South was captured by children's author Annie Fellows Johnston (1863–1931), from her stay with her stepdaughter, Mary Johnston, who lived in Pewee Valley. Mrs. Johnston's observations of the genteel folk of Pewee Valley are depicted in her "Little Colonel" books, which became one of the first international children's series during the time. In the same vein, D.W. Griffith (1875–1948) who was born in Centerfield, not far from Pewee Valley, became enchanted with the southern ideal and aggressively pursued these images in the films he directed. Known as the father of modern film, Griffith became the first to produce epic story lines in motion pictures, often interjecting pastoral and dreamlike settings, similar to landscapes of his native home of Oldham County.

After the Civil War, many Africans Americans left Oldham County for jobs in Louisville, as well as larger cities such as Detroit. Many who remained settled around the LaGrange community to build schools and break barriers from the ties of slavery.

AMOS MOUNT LETTERS

Amos Mount's parents died when he was young, and he became the ward of his Uncle James and Aunt Amanda Mount. Amos Mount (1841–1912) joined Company B, Sixth Kentucky Volunteer Infantry, United States of America, composed of mostly young men from LaGrange and Westport. Although Amos was wounded in 1863, he eventually rejoined his unit and was discharged in 1864.

Below are some of Amos's letters as he wrote them, with the misspellings and dialect typical of young men of similar circumstances during those times.

The following letter was written at Eminence, Kentucky, which served as the gathering point for the Sixth Kentucky Volunteer Infantry. This regiment was organized by Colonel Walter C. Whitaker, a Kentucky senator from Shelbyville. Company B mustered in at Shepherdsville November 1, 1861.

Nov the 7 1861
Shepherdsville, Ky
Dear Aunt
I take pleasure in writing to you once more   I hav bin vary sick cinse I last wrote to you   I a chill and the soar throat but I am most well again   I hav sent all of my things home to you in abox with Jo. Dawkings   Thare is a pair of new shoes in the box st Tell uncle Jim that he ma hav them as I had now use for them   I expect we will leav hear to marrow or the first of next week for Emminance and if we do perhaps I will stop and stay all night if I can get off from the capting   I got your leter from   Mr bonar I was glad to hear from you all   I had my minature taken for you and left it with will Mount   he said he was going up in a few day giv my love to all.

Amos G. Mount

PS do not answer this untell I write A gain as we wont be hear long

I want you to look in my satchel and see if I did not send my gloves and day book in it. your obedient
   Nephew

Amos G. Mount

A letterhead and letter from the Amos Mount Civil War Letter Collection.

In the following letter, Amos's company has begun its journey of active duty. Lee and his company were dispatched to Bagdad to suppress a group of men who were capturing Union supporters and forcing them to take an oath of allegiance to the Confederacy. Originally, a small group of men under the command of Second Lieutenant Will Dunlap was sent to quell the disturbance, but it was met with deadly force by forty or so rebels. It resulted in the first Sixth Regiment war casualty. Lee's company was sent as reinforcements, but by the time it had arrived, the rebels had fled. Whitaker gave orders for the company to confiscate all goods the rebels had left. The company traveled into Owen County looking for the rebels, but without success. Isom Moody was the name of the man who was killed.

Camp Sigel, Dec the 19, 1861
Dear Aunt
It is with pleasure that I write to you all though I hav nothing of importanes.
I suppose you hav heard of our trip to Bagdad   it giv me a bad cole trav in

the night   you said in you leter that I must com up as soon as I could. Well you need not look for me soon for Ð I hav got wiend off from home and I do not now whether I will be at home again until my time is out and perhaps I may never see home again but if I dont I hope I will neet you all in aland wher frinds never part   you said in your leter that you would knit me a pair off gloves   I wish you would knit them if you pleas and send them the first chance   write soon give me all of the nuse   giv my respects to all of my frinds tell John that I heard him hollor when we past through saturday   I saw you all   I was standing on the platform of the cars. hear is some receits theat I had in my pocket book take them and keep them for me

I hav nothing more at present write soon tell uncle Jim that I would like to get a leter from him once and a while any how

dyrect you leter to camp sigel col whitakers sixth Ky regiment car of capt Lee.

The following letter was written at the Battle of Shiloh Church, also called the Battle of Pittsburg Landing. The Sixth Kentucky entered the battle on April 7, 1862. The Sixth Regiment arrived late and was forced into battle on nearly empty stomachs. For the most part, the Sixth Kentucky served as reinforcements, moving around the battlefield to give other companies periods of rest from the fights. The regiment experienced heavy fire from Colonel John D. Martin's company and was forced to retreat at one point. It fell back to the Manse George Cabin, where it received support from the Ninth Regiment, which it had been relieving at the time. Brigadier General Nelson would eventually mount a counterattack against the advancing Confederates, and the Sixth would help in driving them back. At least 103 men from the Sixth Regiment died. Company B, Amos Mount's company, came away completely unscathed. Total Federal losses at Shiloh were greater than 13,000. Confederate losses were greater than 10,000.

April 15, 1862
Battle field of shilo near pitsburg landing Tenn
My Dear Aunt

I wonce more hav the pleasure to write to you all since I last write to you we hav marched nine days on a force march and hav bin in one of the hardest battles that has bin fought. We reached the battle ground Sunday night last after dark and we stood in line of Battle all night in the rain, the fight commenced at day light again. It is a day that I never will for get to see the dead lying ove the field and to hear the groans of the woonded. It was one of the awfulest sites that man every witnessed. I counted fourty dead bodys in one place most of thim we rebels. It woul make the hart of most eny one quiver to see the dead and wounded and to hear the groans of the wounded. Aunt you leter has jest come to hand I asshure you that I we glad to hear form you all as I we getting vary anxious to hear from you all. Aunt you said in you leter that you had read a leter from Wily and that he said the lincolnites wer to try to whip them out. Well I hav only got to say that if he is a traitor to his country I hope he will meet a traitors fate for if thar every was eny thing I hate it is a traitor. Aunt you said in you leter that you thought I made my will. No I did not. It was because I couldent but I hope I soo may. You said that I must write plainer well I write plain as I can for I am now seting away out in the woods by self on the Battle ground. We had nine wounded in our company. I will giv you some of thare names, James Russel, John Foster, Dress Shuck, James Waddsen. for the presnt I will stop. Write soon. Aunt I forgot to tell you about paper. I was vary glad to get it and I hop you will send it often. Write soon and giv me all of the nous you said that I most not join the regulars for I would soon be twentyone. Well I have got out of the notion. Your giv my respects to all of my friends. Giv my best love to Mrs. Raily.

Amos G. Mount

The next two transcriptions describe Company B's movements in west Kentucky and around Nashville. Amos's regiment left Wickliffe, Kentucky, on February 13, 1862, and marched forty-three miles to West Point, Kentucky, where the soldiers boarded steamboats headed for Tennessee to meet other troops in Nashville. Mount's regiment boarded the *Switzerland*, which was a 178-foot-long side-wheeler, as it joined a fleet of twenty other steamboats with soldiers. At a stop in Paducah, Amos witnessed thousands of Confederate prisoners from Fort Donelson passing through on their way to Northern prisons. Amos's unit transferred from the *Switzerland* to another steamer and headed down the Cumberland River. The river was flooded, and the boats had trouble navigating, often tying up to treetops at night to avoid getting stuck.

Mr. Hitt, to whom Amos refers in his letter, is from Oldham County and often traveled back and forth to Amos's company from Oldham County to bring letters, clothes, food and more from the families of the soldiers in Company B.

Feb. 27, 1862
Nashville, Davison Co.
My Dear Aunt

Being in camp this morning I will write you all a few lines. We ar four miles from town. We got hear yeastarday morning. we ar all hear safe and soun. We wer on the boat nine days. We past fort Donelson on the Cumberland river. Aunt, I hav not got time to write vary much. I will write again in a few days. I am writing this to send by Mr. Hitt and he is ready to go. Giv my love to all of my kins foalks.

As the rebles burnd the bridg ofver the river last Friday they left hear the day before we got hear. Some few of them left the morning before we got hear. We will not stay hear long.

Tell uncle Jim that we ar moving the rebels now doble quick

Yours truly,
Amos G. Mount
Nashville Tensee for mrs. Amanda Mount

And the second:

Camp Andrew Jackson
Nashville Ten
Davson Co Ten
March th 6, 1862

My Dear Aunt

Being at leasure this Sabbath eavning I will try once more to write to you all. I wrote to you a few days ago and sent it of by mr. Hitt. I suppose you would like to hear something of our trip to Nashville. Well we left Camp Wickliffe Fe 7ᵗʰ and traveled three days through the rain and mud to get to West Point and then wee took the boat for Paducah.

There wee laid up for one day for further orders then wee left for Nashville. We past fort Donlson wher they hat such a hard battle it is one of the stronges places they had and it is a [mystery] to me how our forces evry took it for they had all of the advantage of them on evry side. Our forces had to clime a hill to get them and they had the river in view for too or three miles I saw some of they tree tops cut off a mile down the river by the cannon balls, we ar now incampt back of the town infull view of it. Thar is about sixty thousand heare now. Aunt I am sory to say that one of our men diede yeastarday eavnint his name was Lankford. He was sick about one weak. I do not know what the matter with him.

Gord was here this morning. He looxs vary well. I see him most evry day now as we ar incampt cloast to geathger. Tell Uncle Jim that I sent him ten dollars the other day by Mr. Add. Hitt and I want him to send me one dollars worth of stamps if he pleas as they cant be had hear for love nor money.

Write soo and giv me all of the nouse of the times. All of the balance of us is well at present. Dyrect your leter to
Camp Andrew Jackson
Col Whitaker six ky. regiment
car of capt. R. Lee
for the present I will stop
write soon
your Amos. G. Mount

FANNIE

The following story is taken from an obituary notice in a newspaper located in the history center archives named the *Western Advertiser*, which was a local newspaper published for the LaGrange community. This article appeared on October 27, 1863, and concerns Fannie, who became a member of Amos Mount's regiment, the Sixth Kentucky Regiment, Company B. The company was composed of boys from LaGrange, Westport and Eminence and was known as the fiercest fighting company in the Sixth Kentucky.

Died,
On the battle field of Chickamauga, September 19, 1863, FANNIE

And pray who was Fannie? Doubtless some one will exclaim, in noticing this little boquet, thrown to her memory.—Well, we will proceed and tell

The *Western Advertiser* contained local news from LaGrange including the story from Company B about Fannie.

you. Fannie's life was an eventful one. The first we knew of her was at Camp "Sigel" [sic]." She came to our regiment [Sixth Kentucky] alone, yes, Fannie was unattended, and nameless, and penniless, and homeless. Her sprightly appearance, for be it understood that she was both neat and tidy, and playful ways, together with her friendless condition attracted the attention and excited the sympathy of our then Orderly Sergeant, the kind hearted and generous Martin L. Boner, who at once gave her a name, a home and installed her as an honorary member of Co. B. So sprightly and so well disposed, she become at once a favorite of the whole Regiment. Though exempt from all duty, the Regiment was never out on a reconnoisance [sic], nor engaged in a skirmish without the presence of Fannie, and without missing a single picket duty performed by Co. B. In our march to the mountains in Kentucky, thence to the Ohio River, our passage by water to Paducah, then up the Cumberland, she was with us and it was her honor to be in at the taking of Nashville.

She was with us on that long and fatiguing march through Tennessee, to Savannah, and upon the battlefield of Shiloah [sic]. She was to be seen wherever the bullits [sic] fell "thickest and fastiest [sic]."

Fannie emerged from that slaughter-field unharmed to follow the regiment through the perils and dangers of the siege of Corinth, and its meanderings in Mississippi, Alabama and Tennessee, thence through Kentucky beyond "Wild Cat," in its chase after Bragg, and back to Tennessee. Poor Fannie, she lived through that fierce and hotly contested fight at Stone River, to fall in the battle of "dead Man's Creek." The same cruel shell that stopped the current of life's blood for the gallant Capt. Peter Marder, Co. G., 6th Ky., and likewise Sergeant Kremer of same company, and wounded private A.W. Wells, robbed Co. B of their loved little terrier, Fannie. So closely were we pressed by the enemy, Fannie was left a mangled corpse upon the battlefield. May we not trust that some kind rebel hand will give her a friendly burial. Peace to they ashes Fannie—long will thy memory be cherished by

Co. B., 6th Ky. Reg't.

THE WELLER LETTERS

The Oldham County History Center archives contain a collection of letters from the Weller family from 1856 to 1936. These letters capture several generations of family history spanning the Civil War, Spanish-American War and World War I. David F.C. Weller enlisted as a Confederate volunteer on July 16, 1861, at Camp Boone. He served as a private in the Kentucky Infantry, Second Regiment, Company C. His unit was part of what was later called the "Orphan Brigade." It was so named because Kentucky's government declined to join the Confederacy and supported the Union cause. Having no source of support from their home state, the Kentucky Confederates had to scrounge for arms, uniforms and other supplies. Also, these units were outlawed in their home state, which made it very difficult for the soldiers to see their families. Soldiers were on the move, and family members at home sometimes had to relocate. Communications were infrequent. Soldiers and their families were overjoyed when they received some word that their loved ones were alive and well. Fellow soldiers also tried to keep track of one another, and their letters were often filled with news concerning the statuses and whereabouts of friends and relatives serving in other units.

David Weller and his friend, Captain John Leathers, helped to organize the Southern Exposition. The Southern Exposition was held in Louisville and was a competition for militia groups from across the United States. These volunteer militias were important in restoring order after the Civil War during the period of Reconstruction.

While David served in the Confederate army, he exchanged letters with several fellow soldiers who shared their war experiences. The following letter, dated July 27, 1864, was received from David's uncle, Jim H. Ellis, a lieutenant assigned to Company B, Ninth Kentucky.

Griffin, GA, July 27th, 1864

Dear Dave
I am in hospital at this place. Slightly wounded in the right thigh. My blanket saved me, the ball cut 23 holes in my blanket and dog tent before it struck me. Tom Lilly lost his right arm at the shoulder. Ike Bryant was wounded through left heel. Charly Ceib through the right arm. Weedman through left thigh. Druary shot in fingers left hand, Lou Miller on the chin, Moore is wounded and missing. I am going to the front Friday, write to me and let me know how you are getting along. Direct your letters to the dept. Col Wickliffe, Lt. Applegate and Mattingly are safe. The last letter I reced [sic] from home was dated May 12th, all were well also need Mollie's photograph. Moses Black is dead. Dick Hast was wounded on the 17th June in right hand severely, Joe Wilson and Crit Holtshousen was wounded near Kennesaw Mountain, both in left thigh. Kim Brissba was wounded in foot at Dawson. Co. B has caught the devil but none killed thank God. Our Brigade has only 450 for duty now, out of 1160 they left Dalton with. Bird Joyce was killed on the Second. Jim Talbot is wounded severely in head, he is at the L.P. Moore Hospital Ward, No. 1 Room B. He wants you to write to him. I am expecting a letter from home [and hope it comes soon].

I will let you know the news. Write soon. Yours

J.H. Ellis.

Turbulence

David Weller served in the Confederate army as a private in the Kentucky Infantry, Second Regiment, Company C, and corresponded frequently with his cousin Ino Weller. On August 1, the first Weller letter was published from Ino to David that related battlefield injuries at Griffin, Georgia. The following letter reveals the hardships of the battlefield but also relays a romantic interest of Ino.

Camp, 4th KY Regt., May 3, 1864

My Dear Cousin
Your kind and interesting letter reached me when I was just returning from the "front." We had stirring times for a short while yesterday. Our pickets were driven in and Tunnel. Hill taken possession of by the enemy. We men "culled out," but lucky for old Weller, they had skidadled before we got half way there. I was very glad that days marching and trouble otherwise was sweetened by your timely letter and I intended to show my appreciation by answering immediately. But, I was too tired to do so till today. And what with drills and parades, they keep a person wearied considerably, although not fighting days.

But to the subject which I delight most to dwell on. My sweetheart has beyond a doubt left me with the "bag to hold open" and I have "given over" ever hearing from her again. You can imagine with what alacrity I accept your kind offer in my behalf I however accept of your description as only suited to your taste, not mine. You did not do her justice as to look and if you tell her the truth when you describe me to her, she will think me a perfect monster. I am an advocate, not so much of good look in people as I am of "good hearted" ones. So much be it said to my credit. And her sweet name, "Agnes" must be rejoiced in by a sweet disposition. I am already predisposed in her favor. And if am only fortunate enough to be accepted as needed, I shall be supremely happy. In your hands, Cousin, I entrust my courtship, knowing that you are more familiar with the "cunnings of cupid" than your humble servant. I shall always thank you for your disinterested kindness to me, as concerns the fair sex. Dear creatures are they not? You are probably not aware of my extreme susceptibility. I hope you are not equally as ignorant of my constancy. Is your lady's visit to the Indian Springs to be of much length? I know you will be lonely until she returns. As I said before, I see constant improvement in your writings. The Lightning's flash is truly severe and must be a "stunner" to those who don't "stand from under." Go in and give them fits when you get a chance.

Dave, you asked me for a long letter this time. I intend to continue writing until I get out of scrap, whether it be long or short. I shall not promise to interest you.

I wrote three letters home today and one of them to Miss Mollie Foreman, sister to Dr. Foreman of your Regt. They are cousins of mine. Besides, she used to be an old flame of mine. I did used to love her excessively. I wrote to sister Tillie and brother Jake and to brother Wes yesterday. I always mention you in my letters. I have not received one from home for so long. I do want to hear from them continually, but somehow letters don't come to me as they do to other people. I tell you Dave, you are the only punctual correspondent I have got. I am the victim of misplaced confidence, trusting in people who won't answer my letters. I am now without a female correspondent. Amongst all of the young ladies you know, cannot you induce one to allow me to correspond with her. It is a great benefit to us young folks. Pick me out a good one and I will give you more than one lift in the letter I write her. I trust to your judgement and know your selection will give great satisfaction.

Rations are pretty low now and we bravely live. If you do come up here as you intend, we will give you a cordial reception. My unit lives "bully" and we always forage about and get plenty to eat.

We do not look for a general engagement for some time yet. In fact, we think the Yankees are really afraid to attack us. I hope they are and then they will have to go back the way they came, and faster.

I heard from Cyrus Weller a few days since. He is in Texas cavalry about Galveston. I forget what regiment. David Weller of Polks Brigade, Clabonnes Division comes over often to see me. Wm Henry Weller, Ordinance Officer, in Baker's Staff, Stewarts Div. Also calls upon me occasionally. Strayfellow and Clarke are fat and send best love. George Beatty is with the Company at present having returned from _ewnau [illegible]. He is not well by any means. He is ordered to report to General _____ [illegible] in Atlanta, General Provost duty, but swears he will not do that—die first.

I will go to town and get that KY Battle Song and enclose it if I can. Charlie Ward is a member of my company and, of course, I got a manuscript copy a long time since. He has sold a great many copies of it already and expects to sell more. I am out of scrap, besides by the time I eat my dinner, it will be drill time, and dinner is a consideration now.

Your Cousin, Truly

Ino H. Weller

Turbulence

In the following letter, the Civil War had ended and David Weller was living in Elizabethtown, Kentucky, looking for work as a newspaper writer. His aunt Lizzie Leeper, who lived in Canton, Missouri, with Weller's grandmother, wrote this letter to David. The Knights of the Golden Circle to which she referred was a very short-lived rebellion group that existed after the Civil War, during the uneasy period of Reconstruction. Some excerpts of this letter have been omitted.

Canton, Missouri July 27th 1865

My Dear Nephew

I received your last letter in due time. Grandma and I were both anxiously looking for it. Sorry your shoulder keeps sore—fear it will not get well. Hope you will get to see us pretty soon. We are tolerably well now, but Mary has been worse lately: never will be well I fear. Such a sweet child she is when half well but alas! Alas! What an affliction. I wrote to your Aunt Amanda: Mr. Johnson looked around in LaGrange [LaGrange, Missouri] *to find a place for you; but none vacant now. I went to the printing office here; edited by preacher Barrett. My* [illegible] *told me they had three hands and only work for four days in the week, work being so scarce. Said he used to know you in the reporter office, and would send you the Canton paper. I hope however, you will find something to keep you when you come. I know you can live here, as well as any place if you are peaceable. I believe you have good sense enough to see that is the right policy. Many bushwhackers are coming home: and some have been committing murder in the back country. The militia are enrolled and ready for them and if any more such things are done they are to be hunted out and killed wherever found; that is the only way to stop them. The most inhuman murders that ever were committed by any people civil, or savage have been done in Missouri. When we had no soldiers here, a band of cut throats came in town at 11 o'clock at night, guarded every corner while some went down to the warehouse and killed Mr. W. Carnagy while attending to his own business. That is and has been the sworn policy of Jefferson Davis and his confederate leaders for 30 years. Let me tell you I have been reading a book called Knights of the Golden Circle by one of their order. Says this rebellion commenced 30 years ago—they were first called Southers Rights Club now K of the GC—they are sworn to kill union people in every shape or form convenient, either by poison, might night murder or any way so they exterminate them—to work secretly and underminedly* [sic]. *At the given time, were to break out all over the U.S. and they'd exterminate the whole union which they did in many places, but thanks be to our heavenly Father have not succeeded. They did not yet get as much help north as expected—neither foreign help: so they could not gain the day. They intended after conquering the U.S. to go to Mexico and there establish a limited Monarchy. But the Almighty did not answer Jef Davis prayers: I always believed this union would stand because the Lord is for the right. Now dear Davie, I do not wish to hurt your feelings, you fought in the cause of the wrong: do not continue with the plotters of treason; come out and shun them like vipers. Your grandma says study it over well, you will see how wrong it it; and that it is manly and honorourable* [sic] *to ask pardon and live here in peace under the best government that was ever on the face of the earth. Do not give up your country and friends, all because you are too stout to apply for pardon. More than that, you are a Christian and doubtedly* [sic] *profess to go by the bible, which tells us to be subject to the powers that be. Our Saviour himself paid tribute when he was on the earth. Turn to Romans thirteenth chapter, there you will see what our duty is and tell me in your next letter if I do not say right. Tell us too that you are now ready to come back to the good old union your grandpa helped fight for. So I will close this subject believing you will act honourable* [sic] *for the cause of God...*

We want to see you so much, and hope you will study well what I have told you and come home to the good old union...

George Leeper is out in the country with Dan Dowel working on the farm. We are by ourselves over since Mr. Leeper died, and but for the wicked rebellion he might be home now and I not have to work and toil for to keep soul and body together as I now do, having to do man and woman's work also...

The sorrow and mourning that J Davis and the other leaders of the rebellion have caused no tongue can tell. One man that went from Canton was starved to death, and others that have friends here were also starved to death. Our poor men put in pens like hogs, nothing to cover them but the heavens, laying in mud and mire, lousey from head to foot, some without a ray to cover their naked up; cold, frozen, starved to death. Ah verily there is a God that saw their beastly murderous conduct. Thousands starved to death by Southern Schibaley [sic]...

If you see Dennis Cutter tell him I am making coat pants and vests in Canton. Go see Mrs. Howel (our old neighbor), tell her to write to me. Inquire what has become of Miss Nancy Hainly, you remember her. Maybe you will see J. Bennet in Louisville. Attend some of our good churches there—keep in the good way and remember we [are] *looking to see you. Is your uncle J. Ellis Wall and the rest of them in Etown well? Lizzie and Henry Newman? also is your uncle quit printing?*

Write soon to your affectionate Aunt Lizzie M. Leeper.

CAMP KAVANAUGH, CAMP MEETINGS AND CHAUTAUQUAS

During the 1800s, camp meetings became popular social events and attracted large crowds. The camp meetings were often communal religious services that were conducted together by Presbyterians, Baptists and Methodists. According to Oldham County historian Lucien Rule, the first camp meeting was held in 1790 on the banks of the Red River in Kentucky. People traveled great distances and set up homemade tents to attend these events. From these camp meetings, the idea of a Chautauqua Assembly arose, which evolved into two-week sessions of lectures, normal lessons, devotional meetings, conferences and recreational activities that included concerts, fireworks and one or two humorous lectures.

Camp Kavanaugh, located in Crestwood, is a camp meeting ground that was established by Bishop Kavanaugh from the Methodist Episcopal Church in 1875. Kavanaugh traveled extensively in the southern United States as a circuit preacher and later bishop. He started preaching in 1823 at the Little Sandy Circuit (Sandy River area) and traveled on horseback to all the churches in the circuit area. In 1854, he was elected bishop.

Kavanaugh, along with T.J. McCoy, purchased two hundred acres near Beard's Station (later changed to Crestwood) along the Short Line Railroad (later the L&N), approximately seventeen miles from Louisville. Kavanaugh and McCoy turned the property over to a board of trustees that obtained a charter and commenced to work under the name of Kavanaugh Camp-Meeting Association. Later an executive committee was appointed to attend to all interests of the association and prepare for the yearly camp meeting. The committee was composed of Bishop Kavanaugh, Reverend T.F. Vanmeter and B.C. Levi.

A pavilion that cost $1,800 was erected from donations, and at the personal expense of T.J. McCoy, a chapel, dormitory, cottages and an enclosed fence were built on the Kavanaugh property. On meeting days, sermons would begin in the morning and continue through the afternoon

A picnic at a camp meeting at Kavanaugh.

People gather around the water cooler at a Kavanaugh camp meeting.

after break for lunch. Crowds would come and bring basketfuls of food, meeting friends and having dinners under the trees.

Usually the speakers were guest evangelists from big cities like Chicago or New York. The following, taken from a Kavanaugh Camp pamphlet housed at Oldham County History Center, is a description of evangelist Reverend

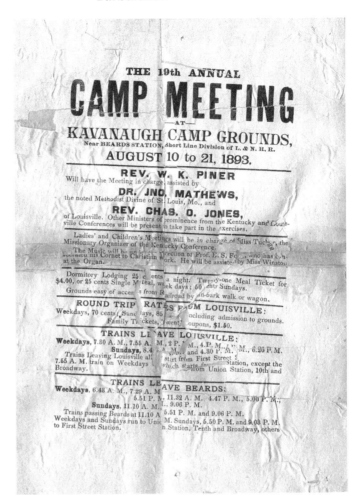

A flyer
announcing an
upcoming camp
meeting.

Henry Ostrom from Chicago, who was the guest evangelist at the camp meeting on the Kavanaugh Camp Grounds August 10–20, 1899:

In the Rev. Henry Ostrom we feel that we have found an evangelist difficult to describe justly without seeming to exaggerate and unduly praise. He is so permeated, controlled and led by the spirit that all are convinced who hear him that with him self is nothing and Christ is all. With a cultured mind, rare natural endowments and a pleasing address, coupled with a consuming love for men, he enchains his hearers from the beginning of his sermons to the end. Fresh and apt illustrations from all the realms of thought, illumine and enforce the great truths he presents: never prosy, never sensational, never verging on fanaticism, but always loving and tender. We wonder not that the hearts of the careless were touched by the score, and that the members of the church were aroused and won to a full consecration and to a larger Christian life. His direct manners, prompt actions and tireless spirit were object lessons from which we learned much that would be of invaluable help in our church work. The results of his ten days' labor were richer than those commonly secured by many weeks of earnest work. The whole church was wonderfully quickened, and among those who were happily converted were young men and women, the middle aged and those advanced in years.

Today, Camp Kavanaugh is still a vital place, and it has hosted various associations throughout the years such as the YMCA, scouts, businesses and local churches. In 2002, the camp went through a major renovation that included the construction of a new conference center, part of which serves as the headquarters of the Kentucky Conference of the United Methodist Church.

ANNIE FELLOWS JOHNSTON AND THE LITTLE COLONEL

Annie Fellows Johnston was a celebrated author of children's fiction from the 1890s until her death in 1931 and is best known for her "Little Colonel" stories centered on old Kentucky's aristocracy and, in particular, one girl, Lloyd Sherman, who was nicknamed the "Little Colonel."

It was while visiting her relatives, the Burges, in Pewee Valley that Johnston met five-year-old Hattie Cochran and her grandfather, Colonel George Washington Weissinger, the inspirations for the characters Old Colonel Lloyd and Little Colonel Lloyd Sherman in the now classic first tale, *The Little Colonel*. Published in 1895, the book proved so popular that more stories soon followed. Though Johnston planned to complete the series several times, her fans compelled her to keep writing. The last book in the series, *The Little Colonel Stories, Part 2*, was published just months before she died. The series' fame reached a zenith in 1935 when Twentieth Century Fox released the film *The Little Colonel*, starring Shirley Temple and Lionel Barrymore.

Many scenes in the Little Colonel stories take place in fictional Lloydsborough Valley—Johnston's pseudonym for Pewee Valley in Oldham County. And many of the characters, homes, businesses and churches in the stories were based on real people and places in the charming little turn-of-

Author Annie Fellows Johnston poses with the real Little Colonel, Hattie Cochran.

William and Craig Culbertson were the models for Annie Fellows Johnston's children's book, *Two Little Knights of Kentucky* (1899), as part of the Little Colonel series.

the-century resort town, where it seemed to the authoress as if all the world were on holiday. In the following text from 1929, Johnston explains how she began writing the Little Colonel series.

Out of the Past

The Land of the Little Colonel, like "all Gaul," is divided into three parts. One lies in the State of Kentucky, one in the Country of Imagination, and one in the dear demesne of Memory.

A thousand times have I been asked, "Is Lloydsboro Valley a real place?" and this is always my answer: You will find it on the map of Oldham County under the name of Pewee Valley, but you will never find it now along any road whatsoever where you may go on pilgrimage, for the years have stolen its pristine charm and it is no longer a story-book sort of place.

But thirty years ago, wandering down its shade avenues was like stepping between the covers of an old romance. One had only to stroll past the little country post-office to feel the glamour of the place and meet a host of interesting characters. In those days the post-office was little more architecturally than a magnified dog kennel, but at nine o'clock of a summer morning it was the social centre for an animated half hour or more.

The smart equipages of summer residents were drawn up in front of it. Old family carryalls loaded with children in care of their black mammies joined the procession, and pretty girls and their escorts on horseback drew rein in the shade of the locusts arching the road.

One half expected to find "Mars' Chan" and "Meh Lady" among them, for the families represented here were sprung from the old Virginia stock and showed their birth and breeding both in feature and in charm of manner.

...Among this street one summer morning, nearly thirty years ago, came stepping an old Confederate Colonel. Every one greeted him deferentially. He was always pointed out to new comers. Some people called attention to him because he had given his right arm to the lost cause, some because they thought he resembled Napoleon, and others because they had some amusing tale to tell of his eccentricities. He was always clad in white duck in the summer, and was wrapped in a picturesque military cape in the winter.

This morning a child of delicate flower-like beauty walked beside him. She was pushing a doll buggy in which rode a parrot that had lost some of its tail feathers, and at her heels trailed a Scotch-and-Skye terrier.

"She's her grandfather all over again," remarked a lady in one of the carriages, "temper, lordly manners, imperious ways and all. I call her 'The Little Colonel' There's a good title for you, Cousin Anne. Put her in a book."

KATE MATTHEWS: ACCOMPLISHED PHOTOGRAPHER

Kate Matthews was one of the first well-known female photographers in the country. During her lifetime, she printed hundreds of photographs, and her work was shown in galleries and museums around the country, including New York's Whitney Museum of Art and in the permanent collection of the Museum of Modern Art.

Kate spent most of her childhood and adult years in Pewee Valley, living in her family home known as Clovercroft. She was one of eight children born to Lucien and Charlotta Ann Matthews. Most of her photographs center on people and places of the Pewee Valley community; she befriended and photographed nearly everyone she ran across, including the town minstrel, Jim Felton, who often played for her, and Abe Parker, a laborer she would hire to pick up her trash.

She had whooping cough as a child that damaged her eyesight and rendered her fragile throughout her life. She could not attend public school, so she was tutored at home. Her father was a camera enthusiast, and Kate became interested in all phases of his photography. Her father, noting her interest, bought her first camera for her at sixteen years of age. It was a large, heavy box with a tripod and had an extra fine lens and a case of glass plates; it was as big as a breadbox. Throughout her life she used this camera, developing and printing her own pictures, long after paper film became available.

In the early Pewee Valley days, she had a cart and pony to help transport her camera and equipment. Her work is characterized by a romanticized scene, and she often had subjects poised and posed, many times reflecting earlier times. Kate's subjects ranged from the people and places in her neighborhood to staged tableaus of author Annie Fellows Johnston's storybook characters from the Little Colonel series. Johnston and Matthews were contemporaries who knew each other and their families. It was Matthews who produced the Little Colonel postcards that are collectors' items today. The following is a vignette description of a Christmas celebration with Kate Matthews's family in the early twentieth century.

Kate Matthews's images often featured romanticized and posed subjects depicting ethereal and dreamlike states.

Christmas at Clovercroft

Christmas at "Clovercroft," the Matthews' spacious home, was always a very exciting and festive time of year. Weeks before the day there was an air of secrecy and much went on behind closed doors for everyone was making gifts. No one would even give a hint so that the recipient of each gift could be completely surprised.

Although the Matthews usually did not have a Christmas tree, the house was carefully decorated. Hemlock and holly were cut from trees on the property and Kate, the photographer, would drive her pony cart into the woods and gather cedar. By the day before Christmas all the pictures, sconces and fireplace mantels were framed with evergreen boughs. The stairway to the second floor was twined with garlands of greens and even the gateposts had their holiday decorations.

Christmas eve the Matthews would go caroling the houses of all their friends. Each year they and the neighbors stopped at Mr. Frank Gatchel's to hear him read Dicken's "Christmas Carol."

Turbulence

The night before Christmas, whenever an adult awakened from his sleep, he jingled sleigh bells. This was the delight of the children because they believed it to be Santa Claus going about visiting the homes in Pewee.

The year that Aunt Jay [Jessie Joy Mathews] *returned from Berlin was the most exciting Christmas. She had been abroad studying piano with Thedor Leschetizky, the renowned teacher. When the doors to the parlor were opened, there was a magnificent grand piano, a gift from her father.*

Another year the husband of one of the granddaughters who lived in the East brought a radio. No one was to know about it until Christmas morning, so in the middle of the night he managed to open one of the parlor windows and put this marvel of the age on a table amid holly and hemlock decorations. Everyone was ecstatic when the radio, one of the first in the community, was revealed.

When Grandfather Mathews [Lucuan Jex] *was unable to plan any unusual gifts he would give everyone a gold coin. A marble top table was draped with velvet and the coins arranged on this. Grandmother Matthews always received the largest gold piece and the others received one of less value down to the youngest member of the family who was given the smallest.*

Before the day of pre-tied bows and rolls of Christmas paper, gifts were wrapped in original designs. The gifts, too, were original endeavors, beautiful handmade creations, embroider, or paintings. Kate very often gave a photograph; one that was especially apropos. The gifts were not opened until Christmas morning and then there was much ceremony. It was a tradition that if you were to say "Christmas gift" to anyone, they were to give you a gift, although you were not required to give one. Since much thought and preparation had been made for this occasion, no one was overlooked and there was a gift for everyone. The poems that accompanied the handmade remembrances were as cherished as the gift, and these were read aloud before the gift was opened.

Often during the holidays friends gathered in the parlor to hear the Matthews' music and to sing the Christmas songs they all liked so much. Jay played the piano or organ; Florence, the piano; Edwin, the violin and Kate, the violin. 'Tis said that Kate never played the violin very well and some would sing a bit "off key," but all joined heartily. When it was no longer appropriate to sing Christmas carols, there were thoughts of the next Christmas.

THE CONFEDERATE HOME OF KENTUCKY

In 1901, the Kentucky legislature introduced an act to support a Confederate Home for veterans who had served in the Confederate army during the Civil War. Many of these veterans had lost their families and finances during the reconstructive period. In 1902, forty acres in Pewee Valley that included the home of Villa Ridge were dedicated by Governor J.C.W. Beckham as the Confederate Home of Kentucky, and an infirmary was added one year later. Governor Beckham's speech included the following:

> *Kentucky must not be considered tardy and neglectful in making this provision for her gallant sons who followed the flag of the Confederacy; for it should be remembered that the soldier of the South, who passed through the terrible ordeal of the war and the far more terrible ordeal of the reconstruction, with his spirit tested in the fire of defeat and suffering, come through it all as a proud and independent American citizen. He has asked nothing but the rights guaranteed him by the Constitution and the privilege of earning by his own brawn and brain an honest living, faithful to his obligations as a man and his duties as a citizen.*

By 1908 there were 348 veterans registered as living at the Confederate Home. Additional land was purchased at the Pewee Valley Cemetery as a burial site for the veterans, many of whom had no living relatives and those others who wanted to be buried with the men with whom they had served in battle. Today there are 313 veterans buried at the Confederate Cemetery.

Many of the veterans had served under John Hunt Morgan, Lee Jackson and the fourth Kentucky Infantry, "Orphan Brigade." The *Confederate Home Messenger* was a monthly publication for the veterans that gave accounts of war experiences, as well as information about upcoming events and news from the Confederate Home. The following is an account taken by Captain Thompson of veteran Taylor McCoy, who was a private in the Orphan Brigade and detailed as a sharpshooter, according to J.R. Hicks and T.D. Bowman:

> *While occupying his position [Private McCoy] in the corps of sharp shooters, he had been shot at several times by an invisible foe. Screening himself from danger as best he could, he scanned with searching eyes the ground in front of him. Looking higher he saw the top branches of a tree swaying gently back and forth. Ah! There was his foeman. Looking through his telescopic sights, he located his man and fired. A piercing cry and a boy*

Confederate veterans pose in front of the Confederate Home in Pewee Valley.

At one time, the Confederate Home had over three hundred residents who came from all over the South. Confederate veterans had no pensions, and many became destitute as they grew older.

fell from the treetop. McCoy, unnerved, dropped to the ground, and when Major Heweitt ran to him, and asked him if he was hurt, he said, "No Major, I am not hurt, but I have killed a boy," adding, "I did not come here, Major, to fight boys, but men." Truly has it been said: "The bravest are the tenderest."

On March 25, 1920, a fire destroyed the main building and west wing of the infirmary. After major repairs from the fire, the home was kept open until an act approved by the state legislature on March 17, 1934, provided for the sale of the Pewee Valley property. At that time, there were five veterans left in the home, and they were removed to the Pewee Valley Sanatorium (which is now the location of the Friendship Manor Nursing Home).

THE CONFEDERATE CEMETERY AT PEWEE VALLEY

In May 1871, Henry Smith formed a group of interested citizens to establish a public cemetery in Pewee Valley. The land was purchased off Maple Avenue and several sections were made. Section III of the purchased area, containing 11,275 square feet, was set aside in 1904 by the State of Kentucky to be used for burial of the veterans who resided in the Confederate Home. Veterans of the Confederate army received no government compensation for their war service since the states for which they were fighting had withdrawn from the United States. Since most of the battles from the Civil War were fought in Southern territories, many Southerners lost their homes and financial security when the South lost the war. The Confederate Home had been established by the State of Kentucky in 1902, prior to the purchase of the burial plots at the Pewee Valley Cemetery, to house Confederate veterans who were indigent, disabled, homeless or had no relatives with whom to live. Governor Beckham of Kentucky and some key legislatures agreed to fund the operation of the Confederate Home if ex-Confederates would raise the money to build it.

There are 313 Confederate veterans buried in the cemetery. Initially, when veterans died, there were annual memorial exercises conducted by the United Daughters of the Confederacy that recognized the passing of veterans that particular year. The services were held at the Confederate Home in the Duke Hall, which was the meeting area. The services followed a standard order described as follows, written in 1906:

Silent Prayers—All Standing
Hymn—"Lead Kindly Light"—Sung by all standing
Reading of the Names of Deceased Members This Last Year
Solo—"Beyond"
Hymn—"God Be With You Till We Meet Again"
Benediction

Often there would be an additional tribute for a particular veteran written "In Memoriam," posted in the Duke Meeting Hall and signed by the Confederate Home officers. The following is a memoriam written in 1934 that honors one of the last veterans who lived and resided in the home.

In Memoriam

Major John B. Pirtle laid the robes of life aside on January 17, 1934. Again the Trustees of the Kentucky Confederate Home bow to the stern mandate of death. The large number of such bereavements experienced by this Board, the vacant chairs we see on every hand seem to remind us "Be ye also ready."

John Barbee Pirtle, Confederate Veteran, was born in Louisville May 17, 1842. He was among the first to enlist when the clouds of war gathered over the Southland. A private in Company B., 9th Kentucky Infantry, he served in the ranks until after the Battle of Shiloh. "Gallant and meritorious conduct" marked him for promotion and he was commissioned in March 1863 for "Valor and Skill." Wounded at Rasaca and Jonesboro he acted "gallantly and faithfully" to the end "in a manner that won admiration from all who beheld it."

As in war so in the busy marts of civil life he followed high ideals. He was a record of ninety-two well spent years. He was always equal to the duties he assumed, a worker quick in thought and prompt in action. Often ardent, always energetic he was yet cool, prudent and wise in counsel.

To the Kentucky Confederate Home he dedicated, with devotion, his time and labor. Presiding over the deliberations of this Board over a period of many years, he gave to the Home diligent, practical and earnest service.

He finished his work. No near relative was left to mourn his passing. His was the handoff affection which led every member of his family to the solemn calm of the grave. Alone he waited for the call which summoned him to the "realm of eternal kindness" where

"His life is now beyond
The reach of death or change—
Not ended,—but begun"
Therefore Be it RESOLVED
    That the Board of Trustees of the Kentucky Confederate Home bear
witness to the worth of this departed member and set aside in page in the
Book of Minutes in honor of his service as President and co-worker.

GLIMPSE OF FARM LIFE IN THE 1800S

One of the oldest English families in Oldham County is the Henshaw/Waters
family, who held the original land deed for Hermitage Farm on Highway 42
outside of Goshen. The family settled there in 1828 and sold the farm in
1936 to thoroughbred horse owner and breeder Warner Jones. Some of the
same family members also purchased Locust Grove in Louisville in the late
1800s and lived there for many years.

    The following, courtesy of Lucy Waters Clausen, is taken from a letter
written by Elizabeth "Aunt Betty" Henshaw on February 13, 1884, at
Hermitage Farm to her sister, Lucy Mary Jane Henshaw Waters, who had
just moved with her husband, Richard Waters, to Locust Grove in Louisville.
George, to whom Elizabeth refers, is George Page, a former slave who was
still living and working at Hermitage. John (who is mentioned to be sick in
this letter) is Lucy and Richard's son.

Feb. 13, 1884
Sister Jane,
    I hear that George Page is to go down to carry some trees, so I suppose
of course, he will go in his wagon, so I have packed some eggs and will
try to ship them by him…and I will write this note to have it ready at any
moment he may go. Though they have such a trick of slipping off without
my knowing anything about it, that he may after all go without eggs or not.
And I surely will be sorry if he for you ought to have the eggs—and I do not
know who else I can get them to you. And if I am fortunate enough to catch
him and send the eggs, for pity's sake do not hesitate to use them up: they
are fresh eggs, packed in meal (the meal is perfectly good) and will poach
or boil nicely. And the hens are laying in the neighborhood of two dozen a
day—that I get—so you see you need not hesitate about using these up; as
whenever I have a chance, I can send you more…

Lucy Henshaw Waters poses with her husband, Edmund. Lucy and Edmund lived at Hermitage Farm in Oldham County, while her sister moved into Louisville and lived at Locust Grove.

I am sorry indeed to hear what a time you have had with Eliza the condition she has been. Your saying that you had no remedies in the house—not even larder rum, reminds me that I had been talking of that very thing, only a day or two before your note came saying that I had just noticed that you had not taken anything in the shape of medicine with you—for as I could see, every vial bottle, box and bundle of medicine was still here; though I had not thought about it or noticed it until that day. That must be attended to whenever you come up; it will not do to be entirely without even the very simplest remedies in the house. I do hope that Eliza's successor may prove more satisfactory than she has done, but good or not or indifferent you will be bound to have someone besides the cook.

Have you had the doctor see John, and what does he think of that vaccination? I really fear that it may be varioloid that he has had. His arm was annoying him greatly when he was here and there was a "waxen kernel" under his arm, but I did not dream of any additional trouble from it. To be sure, if it was varioloid, and he got along well with it—it won't be almost a sure protection against small pox; but meantime, the rest of you might take smallpox from him. And if on the other hand, it was only the result of using impure vaccine matter, it is a pretty strong argument against vaccination.

...Poor Ambrose Larue has another terrible abscess on his hip: I know it would be a terrible grief to his parents if he should die, but to drag out an existence in the suffering and helplessness that seem to be his portion, would surely be worse than death.

Mary has come about getting the washing so I must close and go to her. Your affectionate sister,
Elizabeth

"Varioloid," mentioned by Elizabeth, is a mild form of smallpox usually occurring in people who have been vaccinated or had the disease. Smallpox vaccinations were relatively new at this time in history, so there was a lot of skepticism about the vaccination program.

D.W. GRIFFITH: PIONEER FILMMAKER

David Wark Griffith was born on January 22, 1875, near Curry's Fork in Oldham County to Mary Oglesby Griffith and Jacob Griffith. His father died when he was ten, and soon after that the family moved to Louisville, where D.W. Griffith was exposed to the theatre life of that city. He claimed that his die was cast after seeing Julia Marlowe in *Romeo and Juliet*. He left Louisville in 1897 to move to New York, where he appeared in a number of stage plays. There he also wrote poetry and plays, but his lifelong ambition was to be a playwright.

He went to work for the American Mutoscope and Biograph Company, making five dollars per day as a utility actor. There he was allowed to make one-reel pictures. While with the company, he cranked out some four hundred films and helped to launch some of the greatest silent screen stars—Lionel

Barrymore, Douglas Fairbanks, W.C. Fields, Lillian and Dorothy Gish, Mary Pickford, William Boyde and Eric von Stroheim.

One of Griffith's dreams was to produce an epic Civil War movie. This probably resulted from the early influence of his father, who had been a Confederate officer. He launched the Griffith Studio, and by 1914 *Birth of a Nation* was filmed. It cost $90,000 to produce and grossed $50 million within the next thirty-five years, but Griffith did not profit from the film. He had sold a major portion of his share in order to raise the money needed to produce his dream. This first ever epic film included massive battle scenes and large-scale sets that had never been seen before by film audiences, who up until this time were accustomed to short films that lasted eight to ten minutes.

The Clansmen, the novel that inspired *The Birth of a Nation*, was written by Thomas Dixon and had been an unsuccessful play and even a short

Oldham County
native D.W.
Griffith, pioneer
filmmaker.

Scene from a D.W. Griffith silent film, *Scarlett Days*, featuring Carol Dempsey and Richard Barthelmess.

Scene from a D.W. Griffith silent film, *Broken Blossoms*, featuring Lillian Gish, Richard Barthelmess and Donald Crisp.

movie. The Griffith movie was set in the South during the Civil War and Reconstruction periods, idolizing the Ku Klux Klan as the home guard against the despised carpetbaggers and scallywags. It was certainly a controversial subject, and Griffith had a difficult time trying to get the movie shown in northern cities. Organizations were in line to prevent the movie from being shown until, finally, the mayor of New York allowed the film's premiere. On the first night it was shown, a riot was brewing, and Griffith himself described the scene: "Over the boos, catcalls, and hisses were the whistles and applause. It became a contest. The booers tried to drown out the applauders and vice versa." Rotten eggs and vegetables were thrown at the screen. But the big-screen epic drama, lasting over two hours, caught moviegoers by surprise. It was the first time that people could watch a scene and story line unfold with spectacular drama, and the movie became a successful but controversial film.

During the next eleven years, D.W. became known as *the* pioneer in filmmaking. He was recognized the world over as the "father of film" and was invited to England to meet the queen, which he described as the "greatest moment in my life." He created such filmmaking techniques as the fadeout, the flashback, diffused lighting, moving cameras and high-angle photography. His many films include *America, Intolerance, Broken Blossoms, Orphans of the Storm, Abraham Lincoln, Way Down East, Dream Street, Hearts of the World, Sally of the Sawdust, Sorrows of Satan, Disraeli, Lady of the Pavements* and the first horror film produced, *Avenging Conscience.*

Locally, D.W. Griffith was known as a very generous and friendly man who often came home to visit and walk through the streets of LaGrange. In a 2009 interview with the author, LaGrange resident Ruby Duncan recalls an encounter she had, as a little girl, with Mr. Griffith:

> *I lived at the corner of Washington and Cedar Street. It was a chilly autumn evening.*
>
> *Just about twilight. Leaves were falling. There were several of us that decided we would roast potatoes in the culvert. We gathered some leaves and started a little fire in the culvert. Smoke was curling up and we put the potatoes in the leaves to roast. Then we noticed two men coming down the street. One man was white, the other black. The white man was dressed to perfection down to the spats over his shoes and a fancy cane in his hand. He had a notepad and pencil. They stopped to talk to us. He wanted to know what we were doing. He wrote it all down and laughed with us some. They then walked on down the sidewalk toward the cemetery. Mother came out*

to the front porch and called me in to supper. She said, "That was D.W. Griffith, the movie director, and Dick Reynolds and you kids may be in the movies." I never made a movie but I did marry D.W.'s great nephew, Tommy Duncan. The culvert and house are still there. Even now when I smell leaves burning I think of that evening in autumn.

By 1930, this brilliant filmmaker's career was declining. He married his third wife, Evelyn Baldwin, in 1936 and moved to back to Louisville. He bought a house for his mother at 206 North Fourth Street in LaGrange, and he and his wife spent part of their time at this house, and the remaining time they lived at the Brown Hotel in Louisville. He died on July 23, 1948. He was initially buried in Hollywood, but his grave was permanently moved two years later to the Mount Tabor Cemetery in Centerfield, Oldham County.

ELIJAH MARRS:
PIONEER CIVIL RIGHTS ACTIVIST

Elijah Marrs.

Elijah Marrs was a preacher, writer and educator born into slavery who escaped and joined the Union army at Fort Nelson. He also recruited local slaves to join the Union. He moved to LaGrange and taught at the two freedman schools along with his brother, Henry. At one time, Mr. Marrs said that he had 150 children in his Sunday school class at LaGrange. On November 25, 1875, he helped to open the Baptist Normal and Theological Institute in Louisville, which today is known as the Simmons Bible College. As a politician, he was delegate to every major

The GUOOF stood for the Grand United Order of Odd Fellows. Founded in 1843 by free blacks, it was expanded after the Civil War as a mutual aid society aimed at helping families cope with extreme poverty among former slaves. This GUOOF chapter was located in Goshen and was probably associated with Elijah Marrs's work toward the Freedman Schools in LaGrange, although there is no actual documentation to suggest this at this point.

political convention, constantly promoting African American political and civil rights. He was the first elected African American official in Oldham County as the stump for the Republican Party. He was an activist in voter registration campaigns in 1870, the first year blacks could vote. Shortly after the Civil War, funds became available to establish freedman schools for African American children. There were nineteen schools in Kentucky, of which two were located in LaGrange. Marrs came to LaGrange and lived there for four years to help his brother, who had organized the freedman schools. The following are a few of the excerpts from Marrs's narratives about his experiences in LaGrange:

> *While teaching LaGrange I had occasion to go out into the country one evening to visit some of my pupils and stay all night with them. The latter lived adjacent with some white people by the name of Whitesides. They had never seen a colored school teacher, and from their actions, one would have supposed they had never come in contact with a white one either. They had heard of my coming and were all in the yard of the house, awaiting*

my coming with, apparently, as much curiosity as if I were President of the United States. As I walked into the yard, I heard one of them say, "Thar he is now!" Another said, "Take keer, Ann, let me see him for God's sake!" I underwent this ordeal as I marched down to the quarters of the colored people, the crowd following and stationing themselves about the door of the house when I reached it. Finally, one of them asked:

"Teacher, can you read?"

I answered in the affirmative.

"Well, I wish you'd read some for me."

I took a book and read a portion of it to them, much to their surprise. They were wonderfully astonished that a colored school teacher could read.

During my stay here as a teacher, I was superintendent of the Sunday-school, and for four years did what I conceived a great moral work, among the children, teaching them the Word of God. At times my school numbered one hundred and fifty pupils. I was also secretary of the Loyal League, organized at LaGrange by Prof. W.L. Yancey for protection against the K.K.K.

Part III

UNDERTOW

L ife had changed substantially during the nineteenth century, with technological innovations from the Industrial Revolution that brought new forms of transportation, such as the railways, delivering goods and services to consumers in unprecedented ways. Many people heralded the achievements of science and technology that freed up time from menial chores and tasks that had dominated daily life. Discoveries in medicine and agriculture eliminated the poverty and disease from the past. Electricity, transportation, communication and many other new inventions created the new market of tourism. People could spend their time and money on vacations, movies, sports, shopping, museums and entertainment venues. People could do what they wanted, when they wanted, and spend more time on individual pursuits. D.W. Griffith's contribution to the birth of the film industry is one such example of new leisurely pursuits that allowed people to "escape" into the world of movies, bringing new perceptions of drama and excitement into small-town and rural life.

Small-town and rural life in Oldham County were both affected by U.S. Highway 42, which became one of the major transportation routes in Kentucky, delivering goods and services between Cincinnati and Louisville, as well as connecting these communities on broader levels to markets north and south. Small, family-operated restaurants and motels sprang up that catered to motor traffic. Family farms dominated local economy with the injection of the thoroughbred horse industry, which began to thrive during the Depression. To counterbalance the great migration of populations to cities, the federal government provided new sums of money to organize extension and cooperative services to support farm communities. Large-scale programs were launched to vaccinate livestock for protection against Bang's disease, also know as brucellosis. With the advent of penicillin, dairy farms could expand, and combined with the rich agricultural environment, Oldham County became one of the top dairy-producing counties in the state.

Children were involved in the family farm production, driving tractors at an early age, helping with the family garden, setting tobacco and raising livestock. School vacations and breaks centered on family farm life and production. Schools evolved from the one-room schoolhouse to larger, more centralized locations for whites, but African Americans were segregated into less advantageous facilities and transported out of the county—to Central High School in Louisville or Lincoln Institute in Shelby County—for a high school education degree.

THE INTERURBAN: OLDHAM COUNTY'S TROLLEY

By 1906, a citizen in LaGrange could travel to Louisville on the Louisville & Eastern (L&E) Electric Railroad, "the interurban trolley," with stops along Buckner, Crestwood, Pewee Valley, Anchorage, Lyndon, St. Mathews and Crescent Hill to downtown Louisville. In fact, the interurban had several branches from downtown Louisville that reached to Jeffersonville, New Albany, Charlestown, Okolona, Fern Creek and Shelbyville. The interurban functioned largely as a commuter train, running every hour and speeding along from sixty-five to eighty-nine miles per hour. The cost of a ticket was about one dollar. The train could also pull a small freight car for livestock so that local farmers could ship their cattle, pigs or sheep to the Louisville stockyards. The baggage car could be loaded with milk and cream for shipment to Louisville.

Although people still traveled on trains to Louisville, the electric trolleys were faster. Louisville and Nashville (L&N) Railroad, in an effort to compete with the interurban, created a passenger service called "The Loop." The interurban ran parallel to the rails, and this friendly competition was often not so friendly. L&N claimed to have the only valid deed to the land that its track moved across in Buckner. It claimed to have acquired the land from John Buckner thirty-five years prior to L&E's development after L&E had already laid track parallel to the L&N track. In a 2008 interview with the

ROYAL INN
ROYAL MAGNESIAN SPRINGS
LA GRANGE, KENTUCKY.

With the advent of the railroad and addition of the interurban, LaGrange flourished as a tourist attraction and had five hotels nestled along the tracks. The Royal Inn was a resort off Kentucky Street in Anita Springs.

author, Oldham County native Al Klingenfus recalled a story from his father about the dispute and a competitive incident:

> *Originally the interurban ran from Louisville to Crestwood and decided it was so profitable they would extend the line to LaGrange. That made L&N Railroad mad because a lot of people rode railroad cars in those days* [and they were afraid to lose business]. *So they complained about the interurban going in. So they* [the Inner Urban] *thought the best way to do it was to lay the tracks at night. So the L&N railroad men tried to pull the track—they shot steam on the workers they were laying the interurban tracks. So, the L&I* [Louisville & Inner Urban] *streetcar company put electric on the railroad line, the rail and the whole bunch just fell down, it didn't kill them, but it shocked them so—my Dad told me that, he remembered that. You can see why they would do it—they were trying to come to LaGrange and L&N would try to stop them. Dad actually was there—after shooting that hot water on them, they got them back.*

The dispute between L&N and L&E went to court. Judge R.F. Peak at Shelbyville ruled that L&E must remove all obstructions placed on the lots at Buckner and restore them to the conditions they were in at the time the court injunction was served. Eventually an agreement was reached between the competing lines, and the Electric Railroad was extended.

Unfortunately, the Great Depression and the rise of the automobile brought the decline of interurban use in the community. Bus lines eventually replaced the streetcars, and the lines were gradually phased out.

SCHOOL DAYS AT CENTERFIELD

Centerfield was formerly known as Worth and was established at the junctions of Highways 393 and 22. In 1850, Worth's name was changed to Centerfield, derived from the fact that it was four miles to Ballardsville, four miles to Buckner and four miles to Crestwood, thus being in the center of the field. It was officially declared as a voting precinct by the General Assembly on February 6, 1886. There was, at that time, a general store along with about eleven homes, a school and a blacksmith's shop. There was also a Grange Hall that served as a community meeting place and entertainment center. The following recollection was written by May Barnett in 1974 and describes her experience attending the school at Centerfield in the 1920s:

How well I remember the initial-carved double desks. To have a friend share one with me was great. The temptation to talk often interfered with my need to study. I was often told to take my books and move in with a less talkative tenant.

The big potbellied stove which stood in the center of the room was a source of comfort to us on cold winter days, when we gathered around it to recite our lessons. The coal bucket was watched by the boys. Its refilling offered a means to escape from the monotony of the classroom.

In those days we never heard the words "virus," and we had no fear of drinking from the dipper in the bucket of water that stayed uncovered in the vestibule. We all had colds and runny noses, but that went along with winter. Our freedom was shattered when we began to hear more and more about "germs" and the teacher demanded that we drink from individual cups. Our parents made us wear asafetida bags on a string around our necks. The odor produced by the "wonder drug" overpowered the germs for miles around.

I don't recall much about the lessons we learned, but I shall never forget the games we played. We had a long recess and an hour at noon. We gulped our lunches, which often consisted of biscuit and fried sausage or rabbit. And we were ready to play. We played ball or "ante-over" on warm days and "clap-in-clap-out" when it was too cold to play outside. Those cold days offered an opportunity for the noon Chautauqua where Rozelle and Estelle Brown delighted their audience by singing "Go Tell Aunt Rody."

When the ice was thick on the nearby ponds, our teacher would extend the noon hour and take us skating. If we were not fortunate enough to be the proud owners of ice skates, we could run onto the ice and slide several feet, the distance depending on the smoothness of the ice and our equilibrium.

School entertainments were looked forward to for the Christmas program was given by the students at the church. This was the time when we would recite and sing for our proud parents. There was always a cedar tree decorated with paper chains, stings of popcorn and gum ball covered tin foil.

On Feb. 14th, we always had a Valentine box filled with home made valentines. Bought ones were a waste of money when we could convey our own hand written love messages. The favorite verse ended with "Candy is sweet and so are you."

During the school year there was always an auction. Boxes and pies were sold to the highest bidder, the boys not knowing which girl's box or pie he was buying. This resulted in delight or disappointment since the owner had to share his purchase with the one who had prepared it. We kids looked on with envy, longing for the time when we, too, could participate.

One of these auctions stands out in my memory. A bouquet of flowers was presented to the girl who was popular enough to receive the most monetary votes. A group of young men pooled their money to make Clarence Oldson pay forty dollars to prove that his girl, Martha Sadler, was the "Belle of Centerfield." This won Martha for Clarence and the wedding bells soon followed. I remember some of the teachers: Miss Catherine Cassady, Miss Jessie Turner, Miss Martha Haueter and Mrs. Lindsey Smith.

School Days at Lincoln Institute

Lincoln Institute, located in Shelby County, and Central High School, located in Louisville, were the closest two schools to students in Oldham County that offered high school degrees for African Americans in the first half of the twentieth century. Students who went to Lincoln Institute stayed there on campus through the week because there was no bus transportation available until after World War II. Students who went to Central High School in Louisville could catch the train until passenger service became more limited after World War II. In a 2007 interview with the author, Dorothy Dowe, who grew up in Brownsboro, remembers the early years of segregation and attending Lincoln Institute:

Young women at Lincoln Institute took domestic science classes as part of the curriculum.

Lincoln Institute had sports teams in baseball and basketball for boys.

When I went to Lincoln Institute I actually stayed at Lincoln. It was kind of scary at first living at Lincoln because it was the first time many of us had left home, but we soon adjusted. We could come home on weekends if your parents came to get you. Lincoln was wonderful, we learned more and met people that had had different lifestyles than us. The instructors were college educated and were from places like Chicago and New York. My

Undertow

Lincoln Institute had a girls' basketball team and offered activities such as plays, skits and dances for students who stayed over the weekends.

English teacher was Jennie Hewitt Williams, and I still see her today; we still play bridge together. We had a volleyball team at Lincoln, a drama club, the boys had football, basketball and baseball. They played Central High School in Louisville.

We had a soda fountain at Lincoln and a library and on Friday nights there were sock hops. We usually stayed on campus on weekends; no one had any money to go anywhere. After I graduated in 1949, I wanted to go to KY State but my parents couldn't afford it—that was the only place that accepted blacks, that I know of.

I remember one weekend when I was at Lincoln, Mom and Dad said I could go to a football game at Kentucky State. This other girl and I went and got on the Greyhound Bus at Simpsonville. When we got out of Shelbyville, the bus picked up two white soldiers, and the bus driver told my friend that we had to stand up and give the soldiers our seats. The soldiers said, "No, they don't need to stand up for us to sit down," but the bus driver said, "No they have to stand up," but the soldiers wouldn't sit down. So the bus driver made all four of us, the soldiers and me and my girlfriend get off. So we started walking, and the soldiers wanted to know where we were going and we said Frankfort. So the soldiers said, "We have to go through Frankfort to get to Lexington," so they said, "Come on, we'll walk with you." So we were walking along. Someone came, a car, had some black folks going to the game, and they picked us up.

I think that young people today are not grounded, they are so restless. They need to get closer to their families. I don't think young people appreciate the opportunities that are available for them in getting an education. I felt that the opportunities for me, when I was young, growing up in a segregated society, were much more difficult. I still think young black kids now, still feel that "less than" attitude but not as bad as in my time. I think that in my life, I would have gone to college much sooner, right out of high school.

Note: After Dorothy raised her family, she went to college and completed a nursing degree.

World War I Nurse Hazel Weller

The letter in this section comes from Hazel Weller, a member of the U.S. Army Nurse Corps during World War I. Daughter of David and Molly, Hazel was born in November 1885. Hazel never married. She was employed as a nurse and lived with her mother until she joined the U.S. Army Nurse Corps in

Nurse Weller was a member of the U.S. Army Nurse Corps and was stationed in England during World War I.

1918. By Armistice Day, November 11, 1918, at the onset of World War I, there were 403 women on active duty in the Army Nurse Corps, which was founded in 1901. There were 21,480 nurses who had enlisted during the course of World War I; over 10,000 had served and more than 200 died in service. World War I was a defining moment for the evolution of the U.S. gender system—when women proved they could actively participate in war efforts.

Weller's contribution to the World War I effort was largely in her service with the American Expeditionary Forces in England. She was stationed at Base Hospital 40, caring for seriously wounded soldiers who had been evacuated from field hospitals in the battle zone. While waiting to return home at the war's end,

Undertow

Hazel contracted influenza. She died on July 23, 1919. Many of the nurses, such as Hazel Weller, died from the influenza they contracted while tending to the wounded soldiers.

Sarisbury Court
Hants, England
Dec. 23, 1918

Dear Meenie

Just think only two more days until Christmas. I can just imagine what you all are doing and the fun you are having getting ready for Wednesday. As I wrote Mama—I am still on special and so expect I will spend my Christmas on this case. They are going to have a dance tomorrow night and a tree I believe. I know Virginia Hewitt will enjoy it all very much. Nan wrote me that little Margaret told her about peace—I wish I could see her—am so anxious to see both of them. Have a bib for the baby but seems like I have never leave time to send it, also a few days ago I got an Irish lace collar for her—a coat collar—I asked Dr. Simpson if he thought it would fit and he said he had hopes of her growing.

He liked her picture very much and from what you can see of her face looks very much like Margaret did. This collar I have came from Killarny and I think is a beauty.

What do you think of me getting second prize in a progressive 500 party? Capt. Moran had the party and I came down just to show my face. Did not intend to play but I did and came in second. Miss Pence got the first—a pound note $5.00 and I got 10 shillings $2.50. He said he didn't know what to get so we could get whatever we wanted to. I was so surprised I didn't know what to say. I got another lot of papers today from Nan— hope I get some mail tomorrow and also my box. I have had more fun with my birthday journal everybody thinks it's great! Several asked me how you all thought of such a thing—I said "You don't know my family"!

Some more of the girls came back today—Miss Bryan with them. Nearly everyone is back now. One of our girls went to France today. She got married a couple of weeks ago and instead of sending her home they left her husband in England and sent her on over. Of course she hated to go but orders is orders.

From the latest rumors we will all go there before we come home. Next month we get our first service stripe—one every six months.

We had some very interesting patients to come in a few days ago—they were from Archangel, Russia and had on oilskin coats lined with lambswool. They came straight from the front. It was 20 below there…

Believe this is all for this time and will stop so I can mail it in the morning for if I leave it I wont get to finish it until tomorrow night as I have to read to my patient all day. Write when you can.

> *Lovingly*
> *Hazel*
> *Hazel Lee Weller A.N.C.*
> *U. S. Base Hospital 40*
> *American Exped. Forces*
> *England*

LOUISE HEAD DUNCAN AND THE HEAD TRUST

Oldham County native Louise Head Duncan was the daughter of Peyton Samuel Head and Blanche Hitt Head. She had two sisters, Frances Alley and Margaret Gaines. Louise was descended from the Kellars, Oglesbys, Wilhoits, McMakins, Owsleys and Clores, which were all founding families of Oldham County when it was formed in 1824. Her father, Peyton Samuel Head, started his career as a farmer but began investing locally in real estate and later became one of the founding members of the Oldham Bank at LaGrange.

Louise attended Funk Seminary High School in LaGrange and then graduated from Campbell-Hagerman College in Lexington. She also traveled extensively, including trips to Europe and the Middle East. She had a great

The Head family (circa early 1900s): Francis Head, Mrs. and Mr. Peyton Samuel Head and Louise Head (Duncan).

love of art, history and community, and by the time she died in 1990, she was a benefactor to the LaGrange Fire and Rescue Department, the Harrods Creek Baptist Church Foundation for restoration of its eighteenth-century church and the Oldham County Senior Citizens. She left her family home to the Oldham County History Center for a museum, and she left a trust that has funded many projects in Oldham County in the last twenty years.

Louise had many suitors and was married twice, briefly to a member of the Dodge family though she divorced him and married Curtis Duncan, to whom she remained married until his death in 1963. The following is a love letter that Louise received from one of her suitors, Private Robert Burrell, who was serving in the army in World War I.

Camp de Souge near Bordeaux in France
Dec. 14, 1918

Dear Louise:

The lengthy absence of your wonderful letters continue to exist but I shall in no wise be discouraged in the foolish belief that they will not someday turn up just when I will perhaps appreciate them most.

During the past month my travels have taken me over a better portion of the whole of the French area, finally dropping me in a camp near Bordeaux, with singularly beautiful hope of being returned home at some date in the near future. So far however, I have only the consolation which comes of "hopes."

Very best of health and that my absence on this Xmas from the states will in no wise retard its attendant joys and pleasures that it will share in the most liberal sense it's very blessing wish you.

My Christmas will not be a "joyless" one by any means, and my thoughts will be with you. I am located near Bordeaux, where I hope to spend Xmas day. The spirit of America is here with us and the spirit of the occasion will be universal so that no soldiers Christmas will not be unhappy.

It cannot be denied that it will in no wise be a full Christmas for who does not turn homeward with happy heart in contemplation of the occasion of a "Xmas." The season is a signal not only for sacred commemorations, festal boards, the yule log, but it is the universal signal for family reunions. Therefore a Xmas with vacant places at the family table is indeed not all that the occasion implies.

In my love for you I will share the pleasures of my Xmas and in each of them remember you and wish a million tender wishes from the old world.

Up until November 30th, I had been making my home with Baron and Baroness Laborde at their chateau "La Ragottrie" which is about 10 kilometres from LeMans, France. This glorious place was erected in the sixteenth century. A French countess who has resided there for the duration of the war often took walks with our unit. She could speak English fairly well. Her husband was a private in the Belgium Army and at Camp O'Aunoure (Belgium).
not for from the Chateau. Only the 84th Record Cadre were stationed at the above named place. The Cadre consists of eight officers and ninety four enlisted men.

I may not at the present time recur to any degree of accuracy the places and occasions of my visit to them—places I have been in England, Scotland, Belgium and France. I can describe best in spotless discourse such as would require whole days to write. I shall therefore content myself in this thought and ask you to share it with me.

It will be noted that I am not very actively engaged these days. Before the Armistice was signed, I never had the time in which to write, much less contemplate diversion of any other nature.

Again accept the manifold love of my heart and the wishes I cannot write, except to say merely—I wish you a Merry Christmas and a Happy New Year.

Lovingly,
Bobby

P.S. Will start for home between Dec. 24th and Jan. 1, 1919.

THE DENHARDT MURDER MYSTERY

One of the most famous murder mysteries in the 1930s was the Denhardt murder mystery. (The Denhardt/Taylor Collection, Oldham County History Center, has the information.) Born in 1878 in Bowling Green, Kentucky, Brigadier General Harry Denhardt served in World War I and the Spanish-American War. In 1923, he was elected lieutenant governor of Kentucky, serving a four-year term. In 1933, he divorced his wife of twenty-eight years and bought an eight-hundred-acre farm near LaGrange, Kentucky. It was there that the sixty-year-old Denhardt met Verna Taylor, a forty-year-old widow who was considered to be the most beautiful woman in Henry and Oldham Counties. In the summer of 1936, Denhardt proposed to Taylor with a $1,500 engagement ring, much to the despair of Taylor's two daughters, Mary Taylor Brown and Frances Taylor, and her three brothers, Roy, Jack and E.S. Garr. Denhardt had a reputation of being hotheaded, a womanizer and a heavy drinker.

Three Brothers—and the General's Fiancee

By Bernard Hamilton
Special Investigator for
ACTUAL DETECTIVE STORIES
OF WOMEN IN CRIME

Above: The Garr brothers were tried for the murder of General Denhardt and found not guilty. Actual Detective Stories of Women in Crime *(1937)*.

Right: General Denhardt was accused of murdering his fiancée, Verna Garr Taylor, but never came to trial. He was shot and killed by the Garr brothers as he walked to the hotel. Actual Detective Stories of Women in Crime *(1937)*.

Brigadier General Henry H. Denhardt: His proposed defense at his second trial roused strong opposition

89

On the evening of November 6, 1936, Denhardt and Taylor had dinner in Louisville with friends and were scheduled to chaperone one of Taylor's daughters at a dance later that evening. They left their dinner early because Taylor indicated that she was not feeling well. Taylor called her daughter to tell her that she couldn't make the dance and then asked Denhardt to go for a drive in the hopes that it would make her feel better. They drove down Highway 146 into Henry County and then pulled around to go home. Unfortunately, the car stalled, and a farmer stopped to help them push their car into a nearby driveway, at the home of George Baker. Another man, J.B. Hundley, stopped by to help and offered to go in search of a new battery for the car.

George Baker invited Denhardt and Taylor into his home several times while they waited, but they declined. Baker's dog kept barking, and then he heard a loud gunshot. Baker went outside to investigate and saw Denhardt standing beside the car. Baker and Denhardt then heard a second gunshot. Baker asked Denhardt if he heard the gunshot, and the colonel replied, "Ain't it awful? She was the finest woman I ever knew."

Hundley had returned with the car battery, and all three men began to search for Taylor. They found her body lying in a ditch, an eighth of a mile down the road with Denhardt's .45-caliber revolver lying several feet from the body. Denhardt kept his revolver in the glove compartment of the car. Henry County coroner D.L. Ricketts said that the position of the entry of the bullet hole in Taylor's chest made it seem unlikely that she committed suicide.

A trial took place in Henry County on April 20, 1937. Over one thousand people gathered in the courthouse and on the lawn for the trial with entertainment and refreshments being offered on the courthouse lawn. The trial ended in a hung jury, and a retrial was scheduled on September 21, 1937. On the night before the retrial, Denhardt met with his attorneys at the Armstrong Hotel in Shelbyville to discuss the trial's strategy and then walked to a nearby tavern. Upon leaving the tavern to return to the hotel, Denhardt was gunned down by Verna Taylor's brothers, E.S., Jack and Roy Garr. The Garr brothers turned themselves in and later were cleared of all charges. Roy claimed self-defense, E.S. claimed mental illness and Roy was unarmed.

No one has ever figured out if Denhardt was the real murderer of Verna Garr Taylor. She is buried at the Valley of Rest Cemetery in LaGrange.

The First Oldham County Fair

The first Oldham County Fair was held on July 4, 1933, on the Wood Axton Farm at Skylight. Wood Axton owned a large dairy and thoroughbred racehorses with a three-quarter-mile racetrack located on the farm. The fair proceeds went to benefit Liberty Consolidated School. Wood Axton and William B. Belknap suggested the fair, and the response was met with enthusiasm and excitement. The committee members were as follows. On the executive board: Professor J.P. Pirtle (chairman), Wood Axton, William B. Belknap, R.A. Jordon, Mrs. A.H. Clore, Mrs. John Bottorff Jr. and N.E. Dick. On the finance committee: Mrs. R.A. Jordon (chairman), Miss Viola Klineline, Mrs. W.J. Smiser, Mrs. N.E. Dick, Clyde Pardue, Amos Wilhoyte, Wade Hampton, J.P. Pirtle and Bert Gottbrath. On the publicity committee: William B. Howell (chairman), Mrs. William B. Belknap, Mrs. H.B. Mahan, Wood Axton and Bernie Breckel. For amusements: William Kendrick and Alonzo Adams. For admissions: N.E. Dick (chairman), Joe Gottbrath, Albert Bottorff, Joe Barrickman, Lee Barrickman, Waller Robinson, Will Carter and Richard Adams. For advertising: Miss Viola Klineline (chairman), A.J. Eich, Mr. and Mrs. H.B. Mahan, J.B. Cobb, Miss Evelyn West, L.W. Kerlin, Mrs. Bernard Breckel and Bert Gottbrath.

The Liberty PTA served refreshments and barbecue dinners. Amusements for children were listed as swimming, boating and games. Events included a horse show and races plus a Dog Show, a Poultry Show, a Pet Show, a Rattiest Auto Show, a Baby Show, athletics, a 4-H Club Exhibit and a Homemaker's Exhibit. The stipulations for the Rattiest Auto Show were that the car must run one trip around the track. The athletics included a baseball game, track events (fifty- and one-hundred-yard dashes for girls and boys; sack races, automobile tire races, a javelin throw, shot put, discus throw and tug of war) and swimming contests (best girl and boy diver and fifty- and twenty-five-yard swimming dashes). Mrs. B. Bottorff and Mrs. Catherine T. Johnson were in charge of the 4-H Club Exhibit and Homemaker's Exhibit. Admission to the fair was fifty cents for adults and twenty-five cents for children.

The listing for the horse show and races were as follows:

Morning
Class No. 1: Shetland Pony, any age or sex, to be ridden by child; Race No. 1: Match Race—One half mile. Class No. 2: Best 3-gaited Pony, under 14 hands, any age or sex; Race No. 2: Mule Race—One-Half Mile; Class No. 3: Pony Pair under 14 hands; Race No. 3: Plug Horse—One-half

Mile; Class No. 13: Farm Pony, Any age or sex: Pony must be gentle and suitable for riding to school or general farm use. Pony can be shown with saddle or bare-back. Entries limited to Oldham and Trimble Counties.

Afternoon
Class No. 4: Best Mare and Colt; Class No. 5: Yearling Saddle-bred Horses, either sex; Race No. 4: Mule Walking Race-Slowest Mule wins, Entries were: No. 1: Salt, No. 2: Poison, No. 3. Black Diamond, No. 4: Old High, and No. 5: Splo Jo; Class No. 6: Best Child Rider Under 10 Years; Class No. 7; Best Boy or Girl Rider—Over 10 and Under 15 years; Race No. 5: Plug Race—Girl Riders—One-half Mile; Class No. 8: Light Harness-Stallion, Mare or Gelding—Any Age; Class No. 9: Family Riding Class-3 or more to ride of same family; Race No. 6: Match Race—One-Half Mile; Class No. 10: Best 3-gaited Mare or Gelding, any age; Race No. 7: Mule Race—One-half mile; Class no. 11: Good Hands Class—16 years or under; Class No. 12: Best five-gaited Stallion, Mare or Gelding; Class No. 14: Plantation Saddle Horse (mare or gelding) any age; Race No. 8: Steeplechase—One and one-half miles—Weight 160 lbs.; Class No. 15: Farm mare and Suckling Colt (draft) to be shown in hand; Class No. 16; Best mule colt, either sex (suckling) show in hand.

The fair was declared a resounding success with an estimated 2,500 in attendance. Professor Pirtle, principal of Liberty Elementary, said that the fair proceeds would be used for improvements at Liberty School for the library and laboratory and for music work. One of the most popular events was the Rattiest Auto Contest. There were seven entries, most of which were too dilapidated to make it around the track. Dwight Freeman from Westport took first prize—his old Ford lost its top about three-fourths of the way around the track and then proceeded to lose a tire and "win" on a rim. John McCombs won second place in a 1917 model Ford, and Carl Vogel entered the most "unusual" car, driving a 1910 model International.

GOSHEN GARDENS

The following recollection, as written by Mrs. Helen Belknap Tupper, recalls the days of roadhouses, motels and restaurants along U.S. Highway 42, the main road between Louisville and Cincinnati in Oldham County before the intervention of Interstate 71. This piece first appeared in the Oldham

Goshen Gardens in its heyday. *Courtesy of the* Oldham Era.

County History Center's 2007 book *History by Food, Stories and Recipes from Oldham County Families.*

> *I can't remember the exact date when Goshen Gardens was built. I know it was in the early 30's when the Big Depression was in full swing. The stone was quarried off Land O'Goshen on south Buckeye Lane as was the stone for the new wing of our house on the farm. Local labor was used and I believe the mason was Mr. Guyton. The brick floors were done with paving bricks from Louisville streets, hence the shiny polished surface. The beams in the main room came from an old smoke house, and when the building was closed up for a few days it smelled like bacon and ham. The original plan, which included the smaller building next door, called for an excellent restaurant and a country market for meat and produce—all local. There were also gas pumps in front of the market.*
>
> *I don't know who the early chefs were, but they were mostly unsuccessful, either from lack of ability or excessive drinking. How Daddy found Mr. Willy Lanfer, I don't know but he was the right man for the job. He had trained under the famous Mr. Solger, who catered to society up and down the Mississippi. Mr. Willy promptly pointed out that serving only Land O'Goshen beef wouldn't work since the "non-steak" parts would overwhelm the restaurant cooler. So, Mr. Willy ordered most of the meat from town, and it was always good. I know this because I regularly rode my pony through the fields (too dangerous near Hwy. 42 because of all the trucks and cars speeding towards Cincinnati)*

and Mr. Willy would cook a steak for me as I watched from a stool in the kitchen. He said people were wrong not to salt meat before cooking it. He was known to be stingy, but he was always very generous to me.

The most famous of his offerings was his salad dressing. It was a hot creamy Italian type which Daddy and I found too spicy and hot but everyone else wanted the recipe. The recipe was a closely guarded secret: Mr. Willy's niece worked for him as a hostess and bookkeeper and she tried to learn it. However, Mr. Willy always managed to send her on an errand at the crucial moment and when she returned the dressing was made and sitting in the icebox. Mr. Willy had promised the recipe to Daddy before he died. Unfortunately, when Mr. Willy summoned Daddy to his deathbed, Daddy was out-of-town and so the recipe died with Mr. Willy.

Mr. Willy was a terrible social snob, probably left over from his days with Mr. Solger, catering weddings and luncheons for society. Daddy would stop by his restaurant and ask Mr. Willy how business was. "Wonderful, wonderful, Mr. William! Mrs. Woozit and three ladies (were here)." It didn't matter that they were the only customers—they were the right sort! There were four stools at the counter where one could be served a quick lunch. The hamburgers were excellent and appealed to the trucking trade who knew about them. When they were eating at the counter Mr. Willy would refer to them as "pitiful trade, pitiful trade."

The menu was good but limited—steak, chicken, lamb chops and occasionally fish. This was before the advent of frozen food, so seafood was a little suspect. In fact, the food was good enough to merit several A's from the Duncan Hines travel guide.

When World War II started, it rang the death knell for Goshen Gardens. With gas rationing, patrons hadn't enough to drive to the country, nor did the waiters. In addition, Mr. Willy's legs and feet were bad from all the standing on concrete and brick floors, especially since he was none too slim. And so, Goshen Gardens closed.

BUDDY PEPPER:
OLDHAM COUNTY'S SONGWRITER

Buddy Pepper (born in LaGrange as Jack Starkey) was a composer, pianist and child star during the prewar and postwar eras of World War II. His most popular hit, "Vaya con Dios," is still a recognizable pop tune that has been recorded by over two hundred artists. Buddy began playing the piano by ear and singing as a child. He made a concert debut at age eleven as piano soloist with the Steedman Symphony in Louisville. He appeared on WHAS radio in the1930s, followed by a succession of local appearances that included Louisville's Loew's Theatre and the Kentucky state fair. He moved to Louisville by his teens and began vaudeville sets onstage. "I remember an all-night blockbuster benefit show at the Rialto, when I appeared on the bill with Baby Rose Marie, a big child star then."

By the age of fourteen, he got a big break when he auditioned for a vaudeville act with Jack Pepper (Ginger Rogers's first husband), and Starkey appeared in Pepper's vaudeville act posing as Jack Pepper's little

Buddy Pepper with Judy Garland—taken at her opening performance at the Palladium in 1951.

brother along with Florence Krauss, who portrayed Pepper's little sister. From then on, Starkey changed his name to Buddy Pepper and got a desire to go to Hollywood and perform. This move led to his first movie contract in *That Certain Age*, a 1938 movie starring Deanna Durbin. His best-known performances were in *Small Town Deb* and *Golden Hoofs* opposite his leading lady, Jane Withers. He was also featured in Walt Disney's *Reluctant Dragon*, *Seventeen*, *Men of Boys Town* and the *Henry Aldrich* series. Although Pepper enjoyed being an actor, his greatest love was music, and he began writing movie scores and was an accompanist and arranger for such well-known performers as Judy Garland, Margaret Whiting, Lisa Kirk and Marlene Dietrich.

In fact, Buddy and Judy Garland became lifelong friends, and Pepper gave Garland and her first husband, Dave Rose, credit for encouraging his career path toward composing songs. Pepper even accompanied Garland in her debut at London's Palladium Theatre in 1951. Pepper recalled the opening at the Palladium:

> *Her performance went smoothly until she finished the fourth number. At this time, we were both supposed to exit. Suddenly the audience fell silent and looking toward the mike, I saw no Judy. However, right behind it, there was our girl—sitting flat on her you-know-what, stage center. I let out a howl, as she did, walked over to her and helped her to her feet. The audience started yelling and laughing with us, with which Judy threw her arms around me, gave me a big smack.*
>
> *It wasn't until Judy started to sing her final number, "Over the Rainbow," that I finally really realized what happened. We were on at the Palladium. A baby spot was on Judy—and she'd done it. They started to roar before she'd even sung the last lyric—and as the curtains folded in on the final words: "Why, oh why, can't I?" it was bedlam.*
>
> *We were a bit bewildered by some of the newspaper reviews. They lauded Judy's performance, yet they commented on her weight, her gown, her vocal volume, and naturally, all mentioned her fall. But we knew, above all, she'd been a hit. By noon that day, her four weeks' engagement was sold out.*

During World War II, Pepper was assigned to the Special Services Section of the U.S. Army. He traveled on a twelve-thousand-mile circuit that included Alaska, performing in various army shows for servicemen and servicewomen.

Pepper signed contracts over the years with Universal Studios, Famous Music Company and Paramount Pictures Corporation. He wrote songs for feature films, including "When Johnny Comes Marching Home"; "Top Man"; "Chip Off the Old Block"; "Senorita From the West"; "This Is the Life"; "Sing a Jingle"; "Mister Big"; "The Hucksters"; "The Winning Team"; "Portrait in Black"; and probably the most well-known of his musical scores, for *Pillow Talk*, produced by Martin Melcheris, starring Doris Day and Rock Hudson.

Individual hits written by Pepper included "Don't Tell Me"; "How You've Gone and Hurt My Southern Pride"; "Nobody But You" ; "Sorry"; "That's the Way He Does It"; "Kitten with My Mittens Laced": "The Spirit Is in Me"; "Niagara"; "Serenade"; "Boogie Woogie Sandman"; "Samba Sue"; "All to Myself"; "You Look Good to Me"; "Chant of the Tom'Tom"; "Manhattan Isle"; "Madame Mozelle"; "God BlessUsEveryone"; "I Just Kissed My Nose Goddnight"; "Oldham County Line"; "It's Lonely"; "Hup Two Three Four Blues"; and "This Must Be a Dream."

4-H and the Extension Service

Canning vegetables and meat was a familiar and common activity when Oldham County was primarily an agricultural county. Small farms dotted the landscape, and everyone raised gardens and livestock for the family. In a 2007 interview with the author, longtime resident and farmer Ann Dick shared this story of when the county extension service conducted workshops and offered large-scale canning services for homegrown produce.

> *Liberty Elementary School on Highway 42 in Oldham County was nearly as busy in the summer as during the school term in the 1940s. Ladies from all around brought their garden vegetables to the cannery. The vegetables and fruits were picked, washed, snapped and cut up at home and taken to the cannery for blanching and canning. Huge stainless steel vats were used for blanching the food. After blanching, the food was then transferred into quart- or pint-size tins and sealed. The cans were processed by steam. We were charged a minimal fee, maybe seven to ten cents.*

The extension service provided a home demonstration agent to help organize homemaker clubs, and there was a county agent who assisted farmers with livestock and crop cultivation. Both the home demonstration agent and county agent worked together to provide the organization of the 4-H clubs that were located at the elementary and high schools.

A 4-H float at the Jones-Downey Day in LaGrange.

Lilah Hembree was the home demonstration agent for Oldham County for over twenty-eight years (1940–68). Those who worked with Miss Hembree remember her dedication and hard work with the homemakers and the 4-H youth. She helped organize over sixteen homemaker clubs and provided instruction and assistance with all the 4-H projects, including the annual 4-H summer camps. Below are some excerpts from Miss Hembree's annual report (1940–41), which she was required to submit to the State Extension Service.

OLDHAM COUNTY HOMEMAKER CLUBS IN 1940
Clothing: Homemakers constructed 2,382 garments having a commercial value of $10,497 and at a saving of $6,501.

Foods: Nutrition was the major project [this year] and 3,800 improved practices were reported by club members. A total of 105,013 quarts fruits, vegetables and meats were canned according to approved methods in order to preserve both flavor and vitamins so necessary for health. The value of food canned is $31,564.80. 1,300 non-members were helped with canning and nutrition.

Home Management and Furnishing: Saving due to project work was $3,563 to club members. 933 non-members were helped. 269 mattresses and 269 comforts were constructed by low-income families for their own use.

4-H Clubs in 1940

4-H Club Members have definitely improved the quality of their work in all projects. During the year Oldham Co. 4-H girls have made an almost unbelievable record which, according to Mr. J.W. Whitehouse, State 4-H Club Leader, Lexington, has never been equaled in Kentucky and to the best of his knowledge in any county in any state.

Our 4-H girls record for the past year is as follows:

136 ribbons won at 1941 Kentucky State Fair, 81 of which were blue and 43 red.

7 State Championships were won during the year.

a. Sylvia Morgan—state home accounts

b. Frances Wilhoyte—state room furnishings judge

c. Iris Shannon—State Style Revue

e. Verna Mae Keightley—State Dairy Queen (based on 4-H club record)

f. Shirley Moser—State Food Preparation Champion

g. Mary Ellen Routt—State Clothing Achievement Winner based on all clothing projects

Four National Championships were won during this year:

a. Sylvia Morgan—National Home Accounts Contest

b. Verna Mae Keightley—National Dairy Queen—$250 Scholarship

c. Irish Shannon—National Style Revue

d. Mary Ellen Routt—National Clothing Achievement Contest: $200 Scholarship

Three other girls, Ruby Hampton, Frances Wilhoyte and Dorothy Atchison won 3rd placings in national exhibits or events.

A total of $1,123.75 in premiums, trips, sewing machine and scholarships was won by the girls during the year.

Junior Work

The goal of 100% completions was not reached, largely due to the epidemic of measles, mumps, and whopping cough and scarlet fever during the winter and spring. There were 100% completions for summer project work.

Training schools for the 4-H leaders were well attended and all leaders were outstanding in their work with their clubs. A very high standard was maintained and the quality of work, especially in clothing and home furnishings was definitely improved. 4-H Club members in the county won, during the year, 7 state events and 3 national and a total of 136 ribbons at the Kentucky State Fair.

HOMEMAKER'S CAMP
Sixteen homemakers from Oldham County attended the District Camp which was held at Camp Kavanaugh, Crestwood. Music and reading were enjoyable features of the camp. Handicraft, which was net darning was well liked. On Tuesday night of the camp most of the campers went in to the Iroquois Amphitheatre, Louisville to see "Three Waltzes." This was an experience few of the women could have other times, so it was double appreciated. Other evenings, after the always loved Vesper hour, were spent in recreation. During camp this year the weather was extremely hot—perhaps that was one reason it seemed to be a "quiet camp." Nevertheless, the "quietness" did not in the least detract from the camp; it was restful and everyone thoroughly enjoyed it.

Due to an epidemic of polio no 4-H club members from the county attend the District 4-H Camp.

RECOLLECTIONS FROM THE DEPRESSION

The following interviews are from local residents who recalled the Depression and its impact on the local community. The first recollection is taken from Charlie (Junior) Prather from a 2007 interview with the author.

My mother was Ethel Gowin, and my grandparents were James William Prather and Martha Howard Prather. My mom's folks were Gowins and Richardsons. My dad came here in the 1920s. My mother had sixteen pregnancies, eleven of us surviving. Two stillbirths, and the oldest was injured at birth and I had an older brother who had typhoid fever and then died of pneumonia; he was five years old in 1935 [when] he died. I was three years old.

He got it from spring water he drank from Henry County, somewhere near Campbellsburg—after he died I was the oldest. My brother was George William, then me, then Lottie Mae who died in a house fire in 1957, then Brandon, then Edwin, Doris, Leroy (everyone calls him Pete), then Sue, Margaret, Teresa and Linda and of course Turk and Sam.

Hog killing at the Caldwell Farm in the late 1930s.

I was actually raised on a dairy farm on Elder Park Road that is now a beagle farm—D.C. Clifton owned that farm. We moved on that farm when I was in the fourth grade.

When we were in LaGrange, the big thing was to come to the courthouse at Christmas. They would have Santie Claus there and fly live turkeys off the balcony of the courthouse. They would let them fly down to the crowd, and whoever caught one got to keep it. I don't remember how many they would let fly down, but there was a big fight one time over a turkey and they quit doing it. Santie Claus would give you a bag of candy, which was big back then because it was during the Depression and you didn't get much back then.

Saturday night was big in downtown LaGrange—the sidewalks would be buzzing with people; you could bring a dollar in LaGrange and have a big time. It was a big time. It took fifteen cents to get in a movie and you get a bag of popcorn and coke for a nickel a piece and go to the restaurant and get a couple of hamburgers and a coke and maybe enough for an ice cream cone.

I went to Buckner Elementary—I graduated from the eighth grade, I went there from second grade on. Buckner was a four-room schoolhouse. It was heated with a coal stove, and the students had to keep the fire going and our water fountain was a bucket with a dipper in it. Everyone drank using the same dipper! They started a lunch program there later, but in the early years you had to bring your lunch. Mrs. Abney was one of my teachers and Mrs. Shipp was another one, she was third and fourth grade.

My classmates included Rose Ethel Hall, Doris and David Abney. We had fifteen in our graduating eighth-grade class; that was the biggest class they ever had. Then I went to LaGrange for high school for one year, and then I got a job and quit when I turned seventeen and joined the Navy.

Being the oldest I helped Dad milk cows. I would get up at 4:30 in the morning. Before we got milking machines we milked about thirty cows by hand. Dad would milk about twenty and I would milk about three or four! After milking machines we had about fifty-five. It was a Grade B dairy which meant you had to keep the floors in concrete and keep it clean but you didn't pasteurize the milk you shipped it to Louisville.

We had a big vegetable garden and raised practically all the food we ate. I remember when blackberries came in season we went blackberry picking everyday! Mom canned blackberries, we sold blackberries, made jams. In the garden green beans were the thing—lots of green beans, Mom canned them. We didn't have a freezer, everything was canned.

At mealtime, the table was pretty crowded. All the kids sat on a bench, a long bench that sat on one side of the table. We had a blessing everyday. Dad would mumble through it so fast, I don't remember what it was! My favorite meal was fried chicken. Mom could really fry chicken. It took, usually four chickens to feed everyone. She fried the necks, gizzards, liver, everything. It wasn't very long before they got plucked that they were in the frying pan.

We probably had about thirty chickens. We had our own eggs, the hens would hatch the chicks out in the Spring—we would pick out the roosters to eat. We also had beans and cornbread and oatmeal, we had oatmeal bout every morning for breakfast—and fried potatoes a lot. Dad liked everything fried in lard.

As soon as the weather got cold enough we killed hogs. We salted and cured the pork. We took the bacon, ham and shoulders and cover them up with the salt and sugar cured it, cover it good and put them in a house out back, not a smokehouse, just a shed.

We didn't have a whole lot of toys—we made most of them. We played softball. We would take an old sock where the heel would be worn out of it and stuff the toe full of rags and stuff like that and use that for a ball. We played a lot of ball with that when I was a kid. Once we got electricity and got a radio, I would listen to all the games I could find. I was fourteen when we got electricity. I would listen to the Cincinnati Reds. Wade Hoyt was the announcer; Burger Beer was the sponsor. And I listened to all the UK games on the radio, any sport I could find, I loved sports.

We would also play games like Holy Goaly. We would take marbles and put them in a bunch of them in your hand, and you would guess how many marbles there was and you counted them and how many you missed you would give them to the other person. If you guessed the right amount you would keep them.

With us older kids, my parents were more disciplinary; they took a switch to you but as they got older, they didn't discipline the younger kids much.

My folks were pretty easy go lucky—they got along pretty good.

In a 2009 interview with the author, Ruby Duncan, who also grew up on the farm, remembered the country life when neighbors helped one another.

Feed for the farm animals came in sacks that were printed with flowers. Mother and the other ladies would exchange sacks and match them until they got enough to make a dress. I had a lot of sack dresses as a little girl. During that time you were lucky if you lived on a farm. People killed hogs and cured the meat, and Mother canned all summer long for the next winter. Men went from farm to farm [to help with] *filling silos. Dad would buy pounds of ice for the men to have plenty of ice tea and cold water. Mother would make milks cans full of ice tea. The ladies of the neighborhood made the* [main meal of the day] *at twelve noon. They would ring the dinner bell for the men to come and eat.*

If I had white shoes in the summer, Mother would dye them for me to start back to school in the Fall. One time they would not take the dye, so Mother said, "Well, we will take them to Mr. Hayden and see what he can do with them." He dyed them and I wore them. Mr. Hayden was a "fix it" man. His little shop was behind the Masonic Lodge Building [in LaGrange].

In 1937, the big flood came. People in Louisville were in so much need. They brought people out here and used our school for refugees. We were out of school for some time. When we went back to school the floors that were wooden have been oiled and the school had been fumigated. My Aunt that lived in Louisville walked a pontoon bridge with her family to get to safety. They came and stayed a while with us.

The Dust Bowl was out West in the early '30s. We would get a day of dust in the air. It was such a nuisance. Mother would pull the shades down and cover the windows with heavy towels. It was just another thing to put up with in the 1930s.

The Ballard Brother's store was on the corner of Main and Walnut Streets. I needed some money for something at school. Mother wrapped one dozen eggs in newspaper and put them in an oatmeal box and told me to take them to Ballard Brothers store, that they bought fresh country eggs and I could have the money for what I needed at school. I did and I received enough money for the event at school.

In a 2007 interview with the author, Dorothy Dowe remembered farm life around Brownsboro.

I guess you could say my life was typical of farm kids at that time. We had chores at home, get kindling and wood in, carry water from the spring, particularly Sunday afternoons we would carry a lot of water because Monday was washday. We had to carry up the water from a spring, I recall carrying this bucket of water up the hill to the house. We got all the water from the spring. The spring was about half a city block from the house. We didn't have electricity—I didn't live in a house with electricity until high school. We had an icebox, Daddy got ice on Saturdays from the stores and put it in the icebox. The ice would stay most of the week—I still have that icebox. We cooked on a wood stove. I had to learn to cook on the wood stove.

We were not far from Sleepy Hollow where there were cottages during the summer around the lake. It was sort of hilly around the lake. People came out from the summer and stayed in those cottages. Daddy said it was rich folks getting out from where it was cool in the summertime. We didn't swim in the lake; we probably wouldn't have been allowed to because white people were swimming there. We didn't even consider it.

We went to Worthington for groceries. They had a truck and they would go around during the week and deliver it to the house and deliver sugar, flour, things like that. My closest playmates were some families around other farms. There was the McWilliams farm that had a black family that lived there—that was the Woolfolk family that worked on that farm. The closest church we went to was at Brownsboro Baptist Church, which is the church I continue to attend. The membership is small, around forty-five or fifty people. It's still a family church. When I was a small there were quite a few black people that lived in Brownsboro. My grandfather had a farm there that my sister still owns today.

Undertow

Charles McComb's Grocery store was a good place at Brownsboro—he and my grandfather were good friends. He and his wife Nancy were very nice; they always welcomed us. If it was cold outside, we could come inside and get warm and we felt welcomed there. It was uncomfortable if you went into some places; you felt like you were not supposed to be there.

My parents were very influential in education. They also felt you had to have an education and you needed to prove you were as smart as anyone else. At the Brownsboro Colored School I went to school with the Woolfolks and the kids who grew up over on the horse farms on Highway 42. Our school burned down when I was in the eighth grade, and then I went to the LaGrange Training School. After the tenth grade I went to Lincoln Institute because there wasn't a high school for blacks in Oldham County. At that time we had moved to Crestwood and Dad worked at a nursery for a man named Walter Edds across from Klein's nursery.

Another local resident, Ida Beaumont, recalled the segregation in the "city life" of LaGrange in a 2007 interview with the author.

My mother ran a restaurant on Adams Street [in LaGrange] where we lived. There were six rooms in that house, there were three rooms she used for the restaurant and we lived in the three rooms in the back of the house. The first room was where the Victrola was, and people danced in that room, and the second room, she had a big round table and they played cards on that table and then in the kitchen she fixed hamburgers and chili and all that kind of stuff. The restaurant was open in the early 1940s. It was across from the Kynett Methodist Church. During that time there was the church and parsonage across the street.

There was two black churches, Kynett and First Baptist. Most of the reverends came from Louisville. We didn't have mixed churches back then; services were long. Lizzie Brown was the Sunday School teacher and she played the organ. She shouted every Sunday during service! She was a very soft-spoken lady, she would say, "Kiddies, kiddies, kiddies," so we were surprised when she yelled in church. Some afternoon's they would have programs. The Baptist Church had BYBU for youth so we would go to that, too—it was something else to do.

I went to LaGrange Training School, which is where the First Baptist Church is now. We walked to school, and during that time Professor Cooper was there and there were eleven grades there. Then they cut off the higher grades and people went to Lincoln. I started in the LaGrange Training

School in 1938. They had three teachers and they had quite a few students. There were three rooms. Mrs. Vaughn taught first through third, and Grace Parrott taught fourth through eighth and Professor Cooper taught the teenagers. A lot of the kids came from Pewee Valley. We had used books; we didn't have a library. We had spelling, math and English and history. We had a lunch room. Mrs. Letta Smith cooked. Some of them brought their lunch.

We played ball on the road; we didn't have city water in our house. We carried water from the spring on Second Street. We all had outhouses—no indoor plumbing. Most all the roads around the town were dirt roads. My job as a kid was doing everything, carried water, went to the store for people. They would give us a nickel to go to the grocery store, there was A&P, Krogers, McKenzie, and there was another one, can't remember it right now.

We had chickens in the yard. We had hogs. My grandfather had a farm, Samuel Tinsley, my mother's father. We would live out there some, too. My grandfather raised most of our food that we had for Thanksgiving. He had a big garden and raised green beans, tomatoes, squash and killed his own meat, like ham and chickens. My mother cooked pies like blackberry cobblers, caramel pies. She used white sugar in her caramel pies, and she would brown the sugar for her pies. My grandfather was married five times! And the wife from Cincinnati, she believed in canning and she canned everything, cabbage, everything, so we didn't have to buy too much!

[As a teenager, because of segregation,] *we could go to the movies but had to sit up in the balcony. We couldn't drink out of the water fountain or sit in the courthouse lawn. You couldn't sit at the drugstore for a drink, but you could go in and get it. A lot of times you had to go through the back door. I didn't go in many places. I pretty much did what I wanted to do and just didn't go to a lot of those places. We bought our clothes at Rosenburgs in LaGrange or go downtown Louisville to Watsons. We went to Glauber's dime store and Gatewood's Drugstore. You could go in grocery stores.*

The small community has changed; it's better. I can go anywhere I want to and do anything I want to in LaGrange where when I was young, I couldn't. I always taught my kids that everybody was human, black or white or whatever. I taught them that if you do something wrong, you should pay for what you have done.

Part IV

CURRENTS AND STREAMS

In 1953, Oldham County consolidated the schools, and Oldham County High School became the only high school for students to attend in the county. High school sports began to change as local talent united on one team and began competing with regional schools, including Louisville. 4-H and wildlife conservation camps were major summertime activities for youth, and Oldham County boasted one of the best county fairs in the state with outstanding horse and cattle shows. Agriculture still dominated the county economics with dairy, horses, tobacco and orchard grass as important contributing factors. By the mid-1960s Oldham County had three golf courses, swimming pools and tennis courts.

With the advent of Interstate 71 in 1969, however, agricultural lands were quickly converted into subdivisions—commuters from Louisville could have a quick drive home to the country. Family farms began to disappear into subdivisions. The job market shifted, and the youth from family farms found better opportunities outside of Oldham County. By the late '70s and early '80s, county government experienced growing pains, and large-scale planning and zoning, along with water and waste issues, became more demanding on the local resources. Fortunately, the large amount of green space and park planning has become an important factor for twenty-first-century development, and visionaries have come together to help preserve historic districts within the county's border.

AMERICANISM AND JONES-DOWNEY DAY

On September 26, 1953, the LaGrange Woman's Club sponsored Americanism Day to honor Captain Luther C. Jones and Corporal Earl Downey. Both men had been released from Korean POW camps. Americanism Day was a national observance sponsored by the National Federation of Woman's Clubs. The day began with speeches from local politicians and officials, music by the Oldham County High School band and a parade. Taking part in the parade were the LaGrange Fire Department, LaGrange Rural Fire Department, South Oldham Rescue Squad, Oldham Post No. 39, American Legion, Girl Scouts, Boy Scouts, Crestwood School, Liberty School, LaGrange School, LaGrange Colored School, Pewee Valley Colored School, Oldham County High School, 4-H clubs, FHA clubs, bicyclists, homemakers, American Legion Auxiliary, Crestwood Civic Club, LaGrange Rotary Club and LaGrange Progressive Business Association.

The following was featured in the 1953 *Kentucky Club Woman* magazine and was written by the editor, Elizabeth F. Scheffer.

Pewee Valley schoolchildren participating in the Jones-Downey parade on Main Street in LaGrange.

Sometimes clubwomen get all enthused over a project, but for some reason or other don't do anything about it. Either it costs too much, or it's too hard to get people interested, or perhaps it's just too much trouble, so the project "dies a'bornin'," and the clubwomen forget all about it. But this wasn't the way it was with the LaGrange Woman's Club at all. Definitely NOT! When they decide on a project, all stops are pulled out, and whatever they plan to do is always a big, big, success. At least, that is the way it was with their celebration of Americanism Day.

It all began when the General Federation of Women's Clubs designated September 13–19 as Americanism Week, a week set apart to mark the 166th anniversary of the signing of the Constitution of the United States. Mrs. James Hall, Americanism Chairman of the LaGrange Woman's Club, presented the idea of celebrating the week to her club, where it was received enthusiastically. They lost no time in idle talk. Through their chairman, Mrs. Hall, they contacted all civic and church groups, and all other organizations in their county, soliciting, and getting full cooperation. Extensive plans began at once for the celebration of Americanism Day. You see, real patriotism burns deep in the hearts of people who live in such towns as LaGrange, Oldham County, Kentucky, and in the lush rolling countryside around it.

As it happened, it rained on September 19, so the Americanism Day parade was postponed until September 26. On that day, however, the weather was perfect, and so was the celebration. It was a huge affair—floats, bands, addresses, music, and awards of all kinds. Everybody was interested, and those who did not actively participate in the parade went to watch. All in all, the project was a wonderful success. For one thing, it developed further a spirit of cooperation that always makes for growth in a community, and it brought home to everyone there the realization of what it means to be an American, and to live in this glorious free country of ours.

MALLORY TAYLOR HOSPITAL

From the late 1930s through the early 1970s, Mallory Taylor Hospital was the place of countless newborn babies and tonsillectomies and appendectomies for many of the residents of Oldham County. It was established through the estate of Oldham County native Robert Mallory. Robert Mallory was born in 1851 on a farm about two miles south of Ballardsville off Highway 53. The homestead was known as Oak Knoll, which was an original tract that had

Mallory Taylor Hospital in LaGrange operated from 1937 to the early 1970s.

been in the Taylor family. Mallory was the great-grandson of Colonel William Berry Taylor. Taylor was one of the founding fathers of Oldham County and gave a large portion of property to establish LaGrange in the early 1800s.

Mallory inherited his family's fortune and never married. He supported the local arts in the Louisville area and traveled extensively. Near the end of his life, he decided to leave $80,000 of his estate to establish a hospital in the Oldham County community. Before he died in 1937, he worked with a local attorney, Ballard Clarke, to set up the trust that would establish the Mallory Taylor Hospital.

The hospital at the time was considered to be a model for modern medical practices. Built on six acres comprising the site of a former residence that was destroyed by fire in the 1920s, the home had over fourteen rooms and was nicknamed "Valhalla." The hospital contained living quarters for the superintendent, who resided on-site.

Mr. Mallory requested that all the portraits of the Taylor and Mallory families be displayed in the reception room of the hospital. The hospital had a major operating room, a minor operating room, an X-ray room, a sterilizer room, a surgeon's washroom and a darkroom for developing X-rays.

Patient rooms consisted of two private rooms, five semiprivate rooms, one male ward that could accommodate six patients and one female ward that could also accommodate six patients. On the east side of the hospital there were nurses' quarters, with an additional room for student nurses.

The main floor was constructed with reinforced fireproof concrete, and exterior walls were made of load-bearing tile that was faced with native limestone. The roof was composed of slate-covered asphalt shingles, and the interior floors were covered with asphalt tile to reduce noise.

In a 2009 interview with the author, Ruby Duncan recalled volunteering at the hospital as a teenager.

> *During summer between my freshman and sophomore classes* [at LaGrange High School], *I worked at Mallory Taylor. I thought I would like to be a nurse and worked as a nurse's aide. Dr. Blaydes* [the hospital surgeon] *said some of us could watch him deliver a baby. He said to us, "Now if you get sick or feel faint, go sit in that corner, don't bother me, I can't take care of you and my patient at the same time and don't go out that door either!" The baby arrived and we didn't get sick or faint. Then he let us watch a major surgery. He told us the same thing again. Everything went well and the patient made it. Next we watched him put a steel pin in someone's hip and that did it. I never wanted to be a nurse again!*

The hospital included a wing that was set aside for the use of any aged, indigent women who had resided in Oldham, Henry, Carroll or Shelby Counties; however, there was a special clause that denied treatment to African Americans unless they were kin to the Taylor or Mallory families. Africans Americans had to travel to Louisville for hospital care. Like most hospitals at that time, there were strictly enforced visiting hours, and children under the age of twelve were not allowed in the hospital, even if they were accompanied by an adult.

In the early 1970s, the federal government passed new regulations that made it difficult for the hospital to collect on Medicare insurance. As a result, the board of directors decided to close the doors in 1972. Today, Mallory Taylor is rented for office space. It is located on Jefferson Street behind the Oldham County Funeral Home.

HIGHWAY 42 RESTAURANTS AND ROADHOUSES

Until 1970, U.S. Highway 42 was the main link between Cincinnati and Louisville. This heavily traveled state road meandered along the horse farms and rural landscape of Oldham County. Many family-owned restaurants and motels dotted the highway; the following captures two of the most popular, Ashbourne Inn and the Melrose Inn.

Ashbourne Inn

Ashbourne Inn was a local destination, a restaurant motel in the 1950s known for its wonderful food, as well as a beautiful respite at the junction of Sligo Road and Highway 42. Local Oldham County native Nancy Doty worked at Ashbourne for a brief period. Following is her description, derived from a 2007 interview with the author, of the inn during its heyday.

I married in 1951; I was working over in Ashbourne Inn. Ashbourne Inn was wonderful. Chef Wilson and Wallace Beaumont and Ann Winburn, that is where I learned to eat bologna and peanut butter because Chef said that was the best lunch that ever was and I believed him! And Clara and Jim King, they were wonderful to me and treated me like I was one of theirs. It was a restaurant in a beautiful building that had formal dining room and a gift shop, carried Mary Alice Hadley potteries and really nice gift items. Jim King worked for W.L. Lyons

Wallace Evans Beaumont worked at the Ashbourne Inn on Highway 42 during its heyday in the 1950s. Turkey hash served over waffles was a favorite on the menu.

Brown; he was his aide and I was hired as Jim's secretary, which I really wasn't qualified to do but I tried. I loved being around Clara and the inn, and so when Jim didn't have anything to do I worked for Clara, his wife; she ran the inn.

It was at the corner of Sligo Road and 42 and later on they built a six-room motel, and they had a bridal suite in the motel. They gave little napkin rings that had bride and groom on them, and when I married, I had a pair of them in my suitcase.

It was a destination point—people from Louisville would come. During Derby time and on Monday night they served turkey hash and waffles; they would flock out here for that, that was one of Chef's specialty—he was African American. They served country ham and pompano; that was big, too. He would fix big pots of onion soup; he ran a really strict kitchen. I used to do the inventory. In the winter of 1950, I got up in the morning and there was ice all over the windshield, and so I stopped up here at Albert's [service station] to get my windshield cleaned off, and I started down the road on old Highway 53 on solid ice. I made a complete 360-degree turn, and I was still headed down the hill; if I had been headed home, I would have come home. Well, I creeped along, got behind a sand truck finally, and I drove on in to Ashbourne, and I stayed a week over there. They would send me things over there by cab because the cab took most of the workers from LaGrange, that's how they got to work; so Mother loaded up some things in the suitcase for me and it was nice.

The Melrose Inn

Ann Smiser owned and operated the popular Melrose Inn and restaurant with her husband, Jack, near the Oldham and Jefferson County line. The Melrose Inn was a popular place for good food and a restful night. It was also a great place for parties during the Kentucky Derby. In the following account, Ann provides a brief history of the Melrose Inn and its operation during the 1960s.

My husband and I went to Natchez, Mississippi. And we saw this plantation there which was called Melrose. That's how we named it Melrose, from that plantation. The front of our building looked like this mansion. Then we had an architect to draw the plans—Peyton Davis drew the plans...We started out with thirty rooms. And then later we built ten more, and then we bought Auto Plaza and that added sixteen more—a total of fifty-six rooms. So we operated it all as Melwood.

SINCE 1938

Chicken Trail Inn

"OUT WHERE THE FOOD BEGINS"

Restaurant And Motel

PROSPECT, KY. **Telephone CAstle 8-9983**

On U.S. 42, 13 Miles From Downtown Louisville, Kentucky

From _____

_____

TO _____

The Chicken Trail Inn was another popular restaurant on Highway 42, and it was located near the Melrose Inn. Both the Melrose and Chicken Trail Inns were close to the Jefferson County line and attracted Louisville crowds.

The Melrose Inn became a popular spot and became known for Kentucky Derby parties.

I baked three country hams and made twenty three loaves of homemade bread. And on Derby morning, the day of the Derby, we would serve mint juleps; and we made all those. We minted the bourbon and served mint juleps to all of our guests and country ham sandwiches on that homemade bread and they loved it.

We had a cook, of course, we were open seven days a week, three meals a day, so our cooks from Westport was Bessie Kelly and her daughter, Jerri and then we had Catherine McGrew—she was a waitress. And they would get there at 5:30 in the morning…and then in the evening, we had different cooks. We had a black man from Louisville, Robert Allen. And then we had four black waiters from Louisville who worked for the post office. They wanted a second job, so worked out well. They could come out there in the evening. So we had a different crew at night—stayed open until 9:30—and a different crew in the morning for breakfast and lunch. It was worse than having a dairy. I mean seven days a week, three meals a day, that's a lot. We operated that for sixteen years. That is why I have all these gray hairs.

We were interviewed by the restaurant critics in the Courier-Journal. *And I have a couple of articles that they wrote about our restaurant. And they talked about how cheap the prices were and everything. We didn't charge enough, really. But that is the reason we had a good volume. People start in the restaurant business and I tell them, "The only way you are going to make any money is to give good food at a reasonable price and you will get people to come and you will have a volume." You cannot run a restaurant without a volume of business. So we were able to do that.*

...we had millionaires eating there. Then we had all our tourist trade eating there. And then we probably had truck drivers, and you had to have good food that would attract all those different types, and that was kind of hard to do. Our success was due to our excellent help. Because we did not have a manager for the restaurant, somebody looking over your shoulder. I was doing it and Jack would do some of it, but mostly the employees were operating on their own.

What we sold the most of was a rib-eye steak, a baked potato and a tossed salad. And that was probably our biggest seller. But we had good country ham. We also had good Garibaldi salad and, of course, Derby pie; that's where it all started...this woman made them, Mrs. Kern. She made the Derby pies and we sold them there, no place else...[later] she lost her eyesight and she started making them in her house over in Lyndon. And they would bring them in to our hotel. Then they branched out and started selling them to grocery stores and other places. Now you can buy them anywhere because they are over there in the Bluegrass Industrial Park.

FOURTH OF JULY

The following was contributed by the author, who relates the family Fourth of July celebrations in the 1950s and '60s, when Oldham County was very rural.

We moved to our farm on Highway 53 in 1954, and it had several springs and nice ponds. One pond was spring-fed from an old limestone springhouse. Dad had the bank enlarged and pond drained so when it refilled, it was without fish and always full of fresh clean spring water. Friends and family added a sand bank, dock and diving board. Dwight Freeman, who owned Freeman Ready Mix on Fendley Mill Road, put up a nice shelter, and Dad

Dr. Joe Stearns, Lucille Freeman and Winn Stearns enjoy Fourth of July at the pond on the Stearns farm (circa 1968).

moved the old outhouse from our farmhouse close to the pond so we had all the conveniences! I think we began our first Fourth of July pig roast around 1956, although I am not sure—however, since the '50s our family has had many celebrations at "The Pond," and Fourth of July was always the highlight.

In the '50s and '60s there was actually a pig slaughtered for the event. Although we didn't raise pigs there were plenty of people back then who did. I think Dad and Dwight always managed to get the pig—there were a few times a pig got loose, but it always was caught! Dwight had a large rectangular frame built, and the pig was split and halved down the middle and stretched out on the frame. Lu Freeman always made a "sop" to slap on the pig while it was cooking, which took all day back at the pond. There were a few times when the pig caught fire, due to the negligence of the cookers, who may have had a too much libation with their branch water, but somehow, the pig always tasted great! The firework show, I thought as a child back then, was spectacular. They were not lavish or long lasting, but they sparkled in the reflection of the pond, along with the flashing of the fireflies over the field.

I do remember one particular Fourth, when my brother, Joe Brock, and friend Chuckie Dobbins, who were around fifteen years old at the time, decided they would add to the food dishes by mixing up rattlesnake onion dip and grasshopper brownies. Chuckie had found a specialty store with canned grasshoppers and canned rattlesnake meat. They disappeared during the party up to the farmhouse and made their "creations" then carefully placed them onto the picnic table full of potluck dishes. Of course, they didn't tell anyone the ingredients until all was eaten. People were picking grasshopper legs from their teeth for the rest of the night (or at least imagined it).

JULIA FIELDS:
FIRST FEMALE JUDGE

As the twentieth century moved forward, women's roles changed within small communities. Judge Julia Fields, retired, was the first female judge in the Oldham, Trimble and Henry District Court. Three years after graduating from Yale Law School, Fields was appointed to a vacancy in the district court. The following are some of her recollections, given in a 2009 interview with the author.

Judge Julia Fields was the first female judge serving the Oldham, Trimble and Henry County Courts.

I clerked for Boyce Martin who was a federal judge on the Sixth Circuit Court of Appeals. I did that for three years after law school. [After working as clerk, Judge Fields came to district court, which includes Oldham, Trimble and Henry Counties.]

There was a vacancy on the district court bench when Dennis [Fritz] *first became circuit judge. I applied and was appointed to that. It's the lowest of the judicial levels on the Kentucky court system. Traffic, misdemeanors, preliminary hearings on felony cases, civil cases in which there is relatively small amount of money issued, at that time all the juvenile work was done in district court. That was changed, but at that time all of the juvenile work was assigned to district court. Probate, mental health cases...*

I was probably a little more formal than my predecessor. Although I was enough a child of the '60s, I didn't wear a robe. To be honest, I believe we all like to have the authority that we still thought the trappings of authority were kind of nasty so I just never did wear a robe. Of course in the twenty years that I was there, the workload rose exponentially as the counties grew, especially Oldham County. My schedule, I would travel between Oldham and Trimble Counties each week. There were two district judges. Ones primary office is in Trimble, and one primary office is in Oldham and we would rotate around the counties.

I think I was a novelty. I know I was a novelty. One of my vivid memories of my first month in office was going up to Trimble County for the first time, and it was a very small docket and there was this courtroom full of people. And as I went through the docket, nobody left except the people who actually had a ticket or something of that nature. And finally when court was over, everybody just got up and left. So I asked the sheriff, "Did I miss something? Did these people need to see me?" He said, "No, they had just never seen a woman judge before." So people just kind of turned out to spectate because it was such a novelty. And I was taken aback because it never occurred to me that people would spend the day just to see a woman do her job.

I can recall that especially in Henry and Trimble Counties that in cases involving sexual issues that the sheriffs would get all embarrassed by having me have to listen to this nasty testimony. And they were quite sincerely embarrassed for me because this wasn't for a woman's ears.

In another story, a lawyer in Louisville came rushing out and this was quite early on—and as I said, I don't wear a robe—I was standing in my assistant's office, and he came barreling in and said, "Honey, you have got to re-type this for me. My secretary made a mistake, and I can't submit this to the judge the way it is. Can you retype this for me? I'll give you ten dollars." I retyped it for him and then said nothing and just let him have a surprise when he came into court.

[Judge Fields recalls a candidate stumping for governor, visiting counties and meeting judges:] *I was in the courtroom with the woman who was doing the recording and the only other person in the courtroom was sitting in the jury box* [and] *was a man; however he was an inmate who was waiting to be arraigned. He was not wearing* [jail clothes]—*this was before they had the black-and-white striped jumpsuit—but he was just sitting there in street clothes, blue jeans. The candidate escaped from his handlers and came galloping over—and of course when you come to a courthouse you have to pretend like "Oh, yes, I hear your son is a wonderful quarterback"—that sort of thing. But apparently he hadn't quite done his homework, and he came galloping over past me and past the woman who was doing the recording and waiting until the lunch break was over started pumping the hand of the inmate and says, "Judge Fields, I have heard so many good things about you." And the inmate was just paralyzed. You know, what could I say? Finally the county judge caught up with him, literally took him by the arm and swung him around and shoved him at me and said, "This is Judge Fields." And I am sorry to say the candidate didn't have the good grace to be embarrassed.*

THE CONSENT DECREE:
A DEFINING MOMENT IN PRISON REFORM

The Kentucky State Reformatory (KSR) opened its doors in Oldham County on October 4, 1939. The facility replaced the old state penitentiary in Frankfort that had suffered extensive damage in the 1937 flood of the Kentucky River. Constructed under the social reform efforts of President Franklin D. Roosevelt, the reformatory was originally a self-sufficient facility at which inmates grew their own crops, vegetable gardens and livestock. Sports programs were encouraged, and inmates often played baseball and basketball games against local teams. There was an emphasis on vocational training, and inmates had

KENTUCKY STATE REFORMATORY

Special Edition
of
"THE REHABILITATOR"
November 1943

The Kentucky State Reformatory opened in 1936 and was constructed to be a self-sufficient operation while providing vocational training for the inmates.

opportunities to work on mechanics and various other skilled occupations. There was also a small store in which leather goods were sold that were handcrafted by inmates. Items included purses, wallets and various other products. Eventually, many of the original programs were discontinued, and by the late 1970s, prison reform went through a new era.

In 1979, a class action lawsuit was brought against the Kentucky Penal System under Judge Charles Allen, chief judge of the Western District Court in Kentucky. The lawsuit was initiated through complaints by prisoners regarding the lack of mental health facilities both at the Kentucky State Reformatory (KSR) and the Kentucky State Penitentiary (KSP) in Eddyville. The result of the Consent Decree order improved prison standards, with renovations upward of $125 million by the time improvements were completed, both at KSR and KSP.

The following is an oral recollection from Tom Campbell (taken during a 2008 interview with the author), who was one of the deputy wardens at KSR during the Consent Decree process.

Before [the Consent Decree], *it was what I considered dangerous. We would have 240 inmates, if I remember correctly, in one of the dormitories. A dorm would have four sections, with 60 inmates or so, in each of those sections, in bunk beds, and they were all crammed in there, without a whole lot of space, with a foot locker, and that was it. We would have no more than two and sometimes just one officer, try to have an officer on each floor, but if you didn't have enough, one officer would be responsible in going back and forth. And I remember one officer said they remembered when one officer was put in all three dormitories, was responsible. So the inmates were pretty much in control.*

The restrooms were in the living areas. At the front of the dormitories were commodes and showers. You could go in and out of the bathrooms. Part of the Consent Decree, we were mandated to make each one of those into single rooms. At that time there wasn't any air conditioning, there were open windows, and the heat was just one big blower that would blow into the rooms, so it was very noisy.

In a year or two before that, they had just desegregated. Down in 4, 5 and 6, that was pretty much the black dorms, and all the whites lived together. [Warden] *Harold Black desegregated the facility.*

We would bid two dorms at a time so they would close one down and do that and go to the next one. They did all of them except dorms 2 and 8 because they were single rooms. Those rooms are deplorable. Half of the windows are broken and rusty, and the heat comes down the hallway, and at the top of the door there is a vent that catches the air and it's old concrete blocks and they are just deplorable.

The new windows are sky windows and central heat and air and single rooms, and they completely redid all of that, so it is almost like it is brand new, new duct work and replaced all that. Now inmates are allowed to have their own TV and/or radio/CD player. Before, they didn't have anything like that; there was a TV room and we had a TV committee that would get the TV guide and determine what would be watched.

They have cable, other stuff, but I don't know exactly what they have now. We had a satellite dish for a while, called Correctional Cable TV, that offered packages, and it was paid for out of the inmate commissary fund so the taxpayer wouldn't pay for it; it's where inmates would buy pops, snacks, the profits from that would pay for that. [Note: many other services such as recreational equipment and educational classes are also paid for by inmates with funds from the commissary.]

The defining moment for the reformatory and the department of corrections was the Consent Decree. The judge mandated us, some folks wanted to do, and some folks didn't. Certainly a lot of folks didn't want to see single rooms for inmates, but we had to show them how much it improved security—inmates couldn't get out through windows anymore, they couldn't pass contraband through windows, those kinds of things. The whole ACA accreditation process, mandated by courts, changed our operation, and it's a much more professional operation, formalized our policies and procedures by national accepted standards across the country; we used to operate by memo, now all of the sudden that changed. It was the first time Kentucky had used standards, so the Reformatory was the first facility in the state to become accredited.

TRAIN STORIES

By 1854, railroad tracks were laid, and the train began traveling through Oldham County. LaGrange, Crestwood and Pewee Valley took advantage of this new mode of travel, and hotels quickly sprang up to provide an exodus for city dwellers who wanted a weekend "getaway" in the country. The train was both a local way for folks to travel and a vehicle for long distance. Up through the 1960s, people could still use the train for travel, often riding the caboose and requesting in advance for trains to stop at desired locations. There are many stories regarding trains and travel through Oldham County.

The Klosterman family at home.

Otto Dilly's family lived in a picturesque two-story white framed home in Buckner close to the south side of the railroad tracks. His father was Otto Friedrich Klosterman (1840–1918), who married Johann Henriette Lefevre (1845–1915). Otto Dilly's great-grandparents operated a winery at Buckner for some years; they had a vineyard of their own but bought grapes from farmers in the area. Otto's grandmother, Addie Klosterman Dilly (1872–1955), shared this story with her grandson, found in *History by Food: Recipes and Stories from Oldham County Families.*

> *The L&N railroad track was in front of the Buckner house, with a side track in the same location, the side track was used to shunt trains there in order to let express trains to go by. A troop train was side-tracked there full of Spanish American War soldiers. My great grandmother, Johanna Henriette Klosterman, asked the commanding officer if they could treat the "boys" with some wine. He said alright, but probably with some regrets, since after several kegs of wine there was a whole train full of too happy soldiers, including the engineer, consequently delaying the train for nearly four hours!*

In a 2009 interview with the author, Ruby Duncan recalled traveling by train as a little girl.

> *I think it was about 1936 when I was a little girl and rode the train to Winchester to be with my father and relatives. I would stand at the*

LaGrange depot and wait for the train to come chugging in. Mother would pin a note on my dress with a big safety pin, and it had my name and destination written on it. She would say, "Now don't buy any apples from the man that sells them on the train. He spits on the apples and then polishes them to make them shine. And don't buy a sandwich from the people in Frankfort that sells them through the window of the train. Who know who made them, they may make you sick." I didn't buy the apples or the sandwiches, and I arrived in Winchester with my little bit of money in my pocket. The train had a cattle car way back next to the caboose. The windows were open. You got a lot of cinders in your eyes.

In a 2009 interview with the author, Lizzie Jumper recalled coming to LaGrange as a young girl from Tennessee because of the railroad.

...see they had railroad and these people came up here. My mother started seeing Floyd Allen [who worked on the railroad]. *My mother loved Mrs. Allen* [Annie, Floyd's mother]. *So she just loved my momma. And she stayed with us and helped her a lot, too. The family moved with Mr. Allen to LaGrange, Mr. Allen's hometown, where his parents lived, Preacher and Annie Allen.*

We rode the train a lot with my ma's mother-in-law, [Annie Allen]*; we was small, we could go anywhere without paying* [because Mr. Allen was a railroad employee]. *So they would get us, we called them momma and pa, they would get us and carry us back to Tennessee.*

They were doing it by hand...if anything would happen to the rails, they would call them out up here, and they wouldn't care what time it was. And they would get up in all kind of weather. They'd come and fix that...a lot of 'em would work on the track. So you didn't really know where you would go from one place to the other until they tell you. They had special cars where men would stay. We would go and visit them sometimes, especially up here.

In a 2008 interview with the author, Nancy Doty recalled World War II soldiers coming through LaGrange on the trains.

We would be sitting in Mary Dee's Shop and hear the trains coming...we would all go out and stand on the street and wait for the soldiers, and sometimes it would go real slow, and they would have mail and they would hand us letters and ask us to take them to the post office...that was the days of the old steam engines...and when so you went out you would get cinders all over your face and hair, that was in the old days before the diesel and all that stuff came out.

The Park Hotel was located across from the LaGrange Train Depot. There was an underground tunnel that tourists could use to get to the hotel. The Park Hotel was demolished in the 1990s.

Occasionally, the trains created problems, the worst being a derailment. At 9:00 p.m. on August 30, 1940, the L&N Third 71, a fast freight southbound on the Cincinnati Division, derailed in downtown Crestwood. The locomotive, 323,000 pounds, had rolled over on its side and down the short slope. Built by Alco's Brooks Works in 1927, it was the 1881, one of the 141 heavy locomotives of L&N's 893 roster. It had been running forty miles per hour when an equalizer broke. There were fourteen broken freight cars, but no one was seriously hurt except for a dislocated shoulder in one of the three train operators. It took four days to put machinery in place to upright the 1881. It was then hauled to a south Louisville train shop, and its engine was rebuilt with a feedwater heater. The 1881 remained on the roster until March 8, 1954.

Today, in LaGrange, the trains are popular tourist attractions. Many tourists visit to take a picture of the large trains rumbling through the quaint historic district of shops and restaurants. During the past few years, as LaGrange has expanded, car traffic has also increased, and the town struggles to keep its unique historic charm without sacrificing the safety and volume of traffic that shares the Main Street of the town with a railroad.

BIBLIOGRAPHY

Anderson, Elmo. *Eighteen Mile Baptist Church History.* LaGrange, KY: Oldham County History Center Archives, 1900.

Anderson, Florence. "Christmas at Clovercroft." *Call of the Pewee,* December 1975.

Barnett, May. "Recollections of Centerfield School." LaGrange, KY: Oldham County History Center, 1974.

Bibb, Henry. *The Life and Adventures of Henry Bibb: An American Slave.* Madison: University of Wisconsin Press, 2001.

Bryan Papers, Oldham County History Center.

Collins, Lewis, and Richard Collins. *History of Kentucky.* Vol. II. Covington, KY: Collins & Co., 1882.

Denhardt-Taylor Collection, Oldham County History Center.

D.W. Griffith Collection, Oldham County History Center.

Fortitude Lodge No. 47. *History of Funk Seminary of LaGrange KY.* LaGrange, KY: Fortitude Lodge No. 47, n.d.

Hamilton, Bernard. "Three Brothers and the General's Fiancée." *Actual Detective Stories of Women in Crime* 1, no. 2 (1937): 2–7.

Hart, James. *The Man Who Invented Hollywood: The Autobiography of D.W. Griffith.* Louisville, KY: Touchstone Publishing Co., 1972.

Hembree, Lilah. *Cooperative Extension Work in Agriculture and Home Economics: Oldham County, Kentucky.* Annual Narrative Report. LaGrange, KY, 1944–45.

Hicks, J.R., and T.D. Bowman, eds. *Confederate Home Messenger.* Utica, KY: McDowell Publications, 1999.

Johnston, Annie Fellows. *The Land of the Little Colonel: Reminiscence and Autobiography.* Boston: L.C. Page & Co., 1929.

Johnston Collection, Oldham County History Center.

Kate Mathews Collection, Oldham County History Center.

Kentucky State Reformatory Collection, Oldham County History Center.

Lammlein, D., J. Overstreet, L. Dott, M. Shannon et al., eds. *History and Families of Oldham County: the First Century 1824–1924.* Paducah, KY: Turner Publishing Company, 1996.

Lillian Goldman Law Library. *An Act to Prohibit the Importation of Slaves....* Yale Law School, 2008. http://avalon.law.yale.edu/19th_century/sL004.asp

Marrs, Elijah. *Life and History of the Rev. Elijah P. Marrs.* Louisville, KY: Beargrass Creek Baptist Church, 1979.

Morgan, David. "The Wreck of the 1881." *Trains* (May 1978).

Morris, Rob. *Three Hundred Masonic Poems and Odes.* New York: Masonic Publishing Co., 1875.

Mount Papers, Oldham County History Center.

O'Neill, Charles, ed. *The Rehabilitator.* Kentucky State Reformatory. Frankfort: Commonwealth of Kentucky, 1943.

OTSG/Medcom Historical Program. "History of the Army Nurse Corps," 2004. http://history.amedd.army.mil/ancwebsite/anchome.html.

Parker, F.W. "Died on the battle field of Chickamauga, September 19, '63, FANNIE." *Western Advertiser*, October 27, 1863.

Pepper, Buddy. "No Sad Songs for Judy." *Photoplay* (June 1951).

Reinhart, J.R. *A History of the 6th Kentucky Volunteer Infantry U.S.: The Boys Who Feared No Noise.* Louisville, KY: Beargrass Press, 2000.

Rose, J. *Kentucky's Civil War, 1861–1865.* Clay City: Back Home in Kentucky, Inc., 2005.

Rosenburg, Matt. "Mason-Dixon line," 2009. http://geography.about.com/od/politicalgeography/a/masondixon.htm.

Rule, Lucien. *Forerunners of Lincoln in the Ohio Valley.* Louisville, KY: Press of Brandt & Fowler, 1927.

———. *History of Oldham County.* Vol. I. LaGrange, KY: Oldham County History Center Archives, n.d.

———. *History of Oldham County.* Vol. II. LaGrange, KY: Oldham County History Center Archives, n.d.

————. *The Light Bearers: Home Mission Heroes of Presbyterian History*. Louisville, KY: Press of Brandt, Connors & Fowler, 1926.

————. *Pioneering in Masonry*. Louisville, KY: Press of Brandt & Connors Co., Inc., 1922.

Theiss, N., J. Theiss and A. Zimlich, eds. *History by Food: Recipes and Stories from Oldham County Families*. Prospect, KY: Harmony House Publishing Co., 2007.

Theiss, N.S. "Life as a Sober Citizen: Aldo Leopold's Wildlife Ecology 118." Doctoral dissertation, University of Louisville, 2009.

Weller Collection, Oldham County History Center.

Wilson, Barbara A., Captain. "World War I: Thirty Thousand Women Were There," 2004. http:/userpages.aug.com/captbarb/femvets4.html.

About the Author

Nancy Stearns Theiss is a native of Oldham County and currently executive director of the Oldham County Historical Society. She has degrees in biology and environmental education and most recently completed her PhD at the University of Louisville on the teaching strategies of wildlife ecologist and naturalist Aldo Leopold (1887–1948). Her hobbies include falconry, gardening and sculling on the Ohio River and serving as a volunteer ghost tour guide for Discover Downtown LaGrange Spirits of LaGrange Ghost Tours. She and her husband, Jim, raised their children on the family farm. Theiss has received numerous awards, including the Outstanding Service Award from Murray State University and the Jefferson Award from the American Institute for Public Service. She is also author of several publications and produces a weekly column on local community history for the "Neighborhoods" section of the *Courier-Journal.*